The Cake C

(Haven't you got anything better to do with your time?)

By

Kevin Frazer

DEDICATION

To Chris, for her continued patience and support with my obsessions

Chapter 1
(Visits 0 only 50,000 to go)

I had already cycled over 60 miles and was about to eat my tenth cake of the day before washing it down with more hot chocolate. I was beginning to feel quite sick but was only halfway and had the equivalent number of miles, cakes and hot drinks still to be consumed. I knew I couldn't stop now or the last two years would have been a waste of time.

This was my last chance to prove the doubters wrong. I gingerly climbed back on my bike and headed off to the next stop.

With cake and drink swooshing around my stomach I thought back to that fateful day when I had only recently become a convert to the way of the bicycle and had no idea just how dangerous cake, cycling and an obsessive personality could be.

*****

We had ridden out to the small Norfolk coastal town of Mundesley where there is a choice of at least three cafes. From previous visits, I believed the Corner House Cafe had the best refreshments even though it misses the sea view - although if you take the table by the door you can just glimpse the water by sitting at the correct angle.

Perched at fifty-seven degrees it was clear to Andrew, my cycling friend, that something was troubling me: he was right. We had been offered only small or medium drinks. The small size I understood but without a large option I couldn't see the reference point to tell how big a medium should be. Had a large size proved unpopular or had the Corner House Café lost all their big cups?

As I explained my dilemma to Andrew he interrupted saying that this was the sort of rubbish people wasted their time writing about on social media.

There are three things you need to know about Andrew:
1. He is very thin so should be good at cycling up mountains (although as we discover later, he isn't)
2. He loves anything Italian
3. He is notoriously hard to please so will rant about almost anything

I had innocently managed to set him off on a full-blown rant, this time on the subject of social media, which the whole café was now enjoying. I wasn't really listening as I used to work with Andrew and over the years developed the ability to block out his ranting. My mind had started to wander off into what turned out to be very dangerous territory.

I was a recent convert to cycling so to make sure there was always a good café stop available on every ride I had started to keep a list of my favourite ones. I was now wondering how I could harness the power of the web to share my findings with other like-minded people and even become an internet sensation.

When I got home I logged on to my PC to research blogs. I discovered that:
1. You write about something on your blog which is called a post
2. Lots of people read it and electronically tell their friends
3. Your post goes viral, millions of people read it and you declare yourself an internet sensation.

It sounded simple enough. I always fancied myself as a bit of an author and was looking for a new hobby since my retirement earlier that year.

It was incredibly easy to set up a blog, which Google had imaginatively named Blogger. Without thinking I filled in the registration details and before I knew it I was ready for my first post.

I called the Blog 'Norfolk Café Cycle Tour', the first of many mistakes as even I couldn't remember what the blog was called.

I wanted to make my first post a bit of a tease and set up what was to come so I wrote this:
'Today I'm launching my café cycle ride blog to document my quest to find the best cafes or tearooms in the Norfolk area.

Over the first few posts I will answer the key questions;
1. *Why am I doing this?*
2. *How does my café rating system work? (Is it suitable for other leisure actives such as hiking and chatting?)*
3. *What are my current favourite cycling refreshment stops?*

Each future post will review a local café or tearoom plus share any anecdotes or useful information about the café or ride, so watch this space.'

I sat back and waited for the post visitor counter to whirl into action. As a patient sort of chap, I decided to leave it an hour or two before seeing how many people had read it, or, as we say in blog land, how many 'hits' I had got.

When I returned, the count stood at one and that one was mine.

Action was needed if I was going to be viral by the weekend: I insisted that my wife, two sons and mother immediately read the first post. I also updated my Facebook page.

This strategy proved less than effective as the count crawled up to five. Peter (Eldest son) refused to get involved with his embarrassing father, my mother didn't know how to find a blog and 55 of my 57 Facebook friends were clearly not proper friends after all.

I was surprised however to receive a Facebook comment from my Aunt. Although we had been Facebook friends for some time I didn't ever remember having any contact from her via this media in the past. I had obviously caught her imagination with my new café cycle based enterprise but when I looked it just read 'Haven't you got anything better to do with your time?'

Chapter 2
(Visits 5 only 49,995 to go)

The next day I wrote my first official café cycle review from the trip to Mundesley knowing that the four people who read the first post would be impatiently waiting for the next instalment.

Admittedly my first post had been a little dull but now I had written about an actual café with a curious cup sizing system, I would surely attract many hits.

Twenty-four hours later I viewed the count - eight hits, double my last post. If each post doubled its views then it would only take 20 posts until each one was getting a million visits. I felt confident my blog would soon be the go-to choice for anyone thinking about going on a café-themed bike ride, particularly if they were going to Mundesley. I did worry about how the Corner House Café would be able to cope, especially as many people would want large drinks.

I urgently needed to review more cafés. I checked my existing café spreadsheet: the Earsham Street café in Bungay topped the charts and was the obvious next choice.

As always, I needed to find a guest reviewer to check out the quality of the guest hot drink so I asked Chris if she would join me.

There are three things you need to know about Chris:
1. She is my wife
2. She is a keen cyclist
3. She is reluctant to go too far if the weather looks being anything but perfect

Unfortunately, the weather forecast on the BBC was not promising so I instigated a three-point plan to get her to come along.
1. We would go on the train, so we had the wind behind all the way back

2. I would lie about the weather forecast
3. I would lie about how far it was

With the help of my three-point plan we found ourselves on the train to Lowestoft.

Every time I had previously been back to a highly-rated cafe it had always disappointed, dropped down the ratings and left me embarrassed after the big sell I had given to my cycling guests. I was relieved this did not happen today as Chris agreed it was an excellent stop, even if she was surprised when it rained all the way back.

Once home, I dried off and wrote up the post, which this time included an actual photo.

As with previous posts it soon clicked up, now by five (mother, wife, youngest son, sister in law and a mystery Facebook friend) but then nothing. There was certainly no sign of anyone I didn't know coming across my work. It appeared there was more to this going viral lark than just putting it out there.

*****

Before I had retired, my work in Corporate Big Business had taught me how important it was to document things, in case you were audited. I wasn't sure why my blog might attract the attention of the café cycle auditors but I didn't want to take the risk.

So I posted the rules.

What qualifies as a cafe or tearoom?
*   It must be independent and not be part of a chain.
*   If it is part of an attraction or garden centre, then there mustn't be an entrance fee to get into the cafe.
*   It must have at least one homemade type of cake on offer.

The five factors measured are:

1. Hot chocolate quality. (HCQ)

I look for a thick drink that has a distinctly chocolatey taste. The most common issue is when the focus has mistakenly been put on the HOT rather than the CHOCOLATE part. A nuclear thermal anaemic drink, where the chocolate powder has been sprinkled onto scalding milk won't do.

2. Guest hot drink quality. (GHDQ)

My cycling guest (or guests) get to rate their hot drink (soft drinks don't count). There is more inconsistency here as the type of drink and reviewer is much more variable. But it is rare for there to be a big difference between the HCQ and GHDQ and if there is I probe my guest further on their rating basis to try and get consistency. Again, the temperature, strength and flavour are the key factors. Controversially I have put a ceiling score of seven for tea as at the end of the day it is just a cup of tea so could never justify a higher mark.

3. Effective cake selection. (ECS)

The number of homemade style cakes (e.g. nothing in a plastic wrapper) are reviewed and factored against how many I am tempted by to give the **effective** cake selection (ECS) score. There is no absolute algorithm thus allowing for adjustments on just how tasty and desirable the selection looks. Having four or five cakes I fancy, and am choosing between, would give a high score.

4. Cake Taste Quality. (CTQ)

Straightforward score of how good the cake tastes. If my cycling guest has also had cake then we agree a combined rating, although if there is any disagreement my decision is final.

5. Ambience and atmosphere. (AAA)

Whilst sitting enjoying our refreshments we agree an AAA mark based on factors like view, noise, space, layout, feel, cycle friendliness etc.

Each category is rated out of ten and the average score gives an overall cafe or tearoom rating. I score the cafe on every visit but to keep ratings current only the most recent three scores count. For further consistency, once rated, I moderate the cafe against others with a similar mark.

It has often been suggested that I rate other items like service, price, toilets, other food etc. but as cake and hot chocolate are the main things I require from my refreshment stop then I don't want other factors to influence the overall rating. If my guests want other stuff scored I suggest they do their own spreadsheet and blog, which I will happily read (to date no one has).

With four entries now on the blog I felt the foundations were in place for the Norfolk Café Cycle Tour blog to take off. Eighteen months later, when I was cycling full speed across Norfolk in the hope of getting my blog mentioned on TV, I realised just how desperate I had become.

Chapter 3
(Visits to date 23 only 49,977 to go)

I had arranged another cycle and train combination with a trip to Cambridge, which would expand the world of café cycling beyond the boundaries of Norfolk. I would thus become a national cafe cycle reviewer with all the (yet to be identified) opportunities that brings.

I was accompanied by another of my regular cycling guests: Big George.

There are three things you need to know about Big George:
1. He is Scottish so it is hard to understand what he is saying
2. He loves beer, rugby, cycling and hoovering
3. He is not actually that big

The cycling part of the trip went smoothly until we got to the café stop. The Tearooms were Victorian-themed right down to the staff dressed up in period costume, a pink-based décor and a jam counter.

Once through the door it took some persuasion to get the Lycra-clad Big George not to walk out as his head was already to start to spin and I could see how uncomfortable he was feeling. Just as he was calming down the costumed waiter came over to take our order. I asked him for hot chocolate, a cheese scone and chocolate cake. Still struggling with the rift in his reality Big George ordered a pot of tea (and cheese scone) rather than his normal cappuccino. I asked him why and he explained in a low whisper that he didn't think they had cappuccino in the 19th century (despite it being on the menu). Things only got worse when his tea turned up on a full china tea service and he started calling me vicar. We quickly finished our refreshments and headed back to our bikes.

Big George works part time and so Mrs Big George expects him to take charge of household chores as she goes to work every day. On the ride home Big George announced that he had a deadline, needing to get back in time to buy a new hoover and clean the house before guests arrived. This led to an enjoyable chat comparing notes and tips on which we thought the best cleaner was and our personal vacuuming experiences with Big George deciding a purple ball Dyson was his best bet. I looked forward to a hoovering update on our next ride.

*****

As I continued to increase the number of café visits I also wanted to expand my cycling guest pool so I contacted old friends Barry and Helen to join me on my next café cycle review.

There are three things you need to know about Barry and Helen:
1. They love cycling
2. They love beer and fry ups, but only as part of a cycle ride
3. They ride a tandem

Barry and Helen and their tandem had been on many adventures in many countries so I thought it was time that they had a café cycle adventure. I had chosen the Box Tree Café in Brooke for this trip.

It was a pretty uneventful ride, if cold, and apart from a quick puncture stop we arrived at the cafe in good time. As Barry and Helen are tandem riders I had made it clear to them that they would only get one vote in the guest hot drink ratings due to my one bike one vote rule (later rescinded).

The high-quality drinks, cakes and friendly staff made this a lovely cosy stop especially on such a cold day. I casually brought up the subject of the blog with Barry and Helen. Helen confirmed that she had seen every post. What about Barry? "I don't get it," he said. "Why would anyone, especially me, want to read about your cycle rides and what cake you ate. Haven't people got better things to do with their time?"

I protested. "What is currently the fastest growing sport in the UK?" I asked. Barry got out his smart phone and a quick Google later announced it was Triathlon. "Exactly", I said "That's a sport with lots of cycling so people are mad for cycle-related stuff. And what is the fastest growing hobby?"

Before he had a chance to Google this I confidently said that thanks to the Great British Bake off it was home baking (though I had no evidence). "Therefore, the combination of bikes and cakes is going to be irresistible to the British public and I'm convinced they will soon coming flocking to my blog," I told him.

Barry considered this for a few seconds. "Rubbish" he said, "It doesn't work like that". People like cars and football but you wouldn't combine them into a blog about what happens when you drive to different grounds." I thought it sounded like an excellent topic for a blog, especially if you included route information and rated the half time pies but that wasn't the point.

"You just don't get the world of social media" I said. "I'm sure my blog will be a big success, you just wait. I've had nearly a hundred visits already - that's nearly fifteen a week".

"Yes, but it's only people you know who are being supportive as they feel sorry for you. I'm sure they will soon get bored and the whole thing will dry up," Barry said.

"OK then. I bet the blog will still be going strong after two years with an increasing readership".

"No, it won't" he said. "How can you keep people interested in stories about riding a bike and eating cake. Reading it once, not that I have, might be vaguely amusing but the novelty will soon wear off".

"It won't" I said "and we will ride again after two years of the blog where you can admit you were wrong. It won't be cake but humble pie for you that day". I got out my phone and added an appointment to my diary for October in two years' time: "Invited Barry on ride to eat humble pie".

Chapter 4
(Visits 87 only 49,913 to go)

Now it had got personal, I wanted a real banker for my next trip so headed out to another one of my favourite cafes. Tabnabs in Mattishall, another small Norfolk village, had always delivered an excellent cake and drinks experience. I had particularly enjoyed the chocolate and beetroot cake on my last visit so opted to take Chris as she is a big fan of chocolate. When we arrived, I ordered Chris the chocolate and beetroot cake and myself some lemon and courgette. On the cakes arrival she turned her nose up, saying she couldn't bring herself to eat a root vegetable-based cake, so I was a little surprised when she got herself some carrot cake instead. It was good news for me as I now had two bits of cake to eat making up 3 of my 5 a day.

More research of other blogs had suggested pictures might help attract punters to my site. I decided that as a minimum I would always include a photo of the café or tearoom being reviewed, cake selection and drinks in every post. Exciting stuff!

With this in mind I undertook two rides out to the small town of Reepham, one planned and one not. I discovered that Reepham has two old railway stations, one to the south (Whitwell) and one to the North (Reepham). It is hard to see how a very small town of this size would ever have needed this much transport infrastructure, unless of course it had been planning to hold a major sporting event, but I had no recollection of the Reepham Olympic or World Cup bid. Both the stations have long since been axed from the rail network so one is now on a cycle path and the other has steam trains to visit.

The first ride was to the Northern station on the Marriott's Way cycle path. I would also use this trip as an opportunity to try out my new Alarmio security lock that I had purchased on an online auction site from somewhere in the Far East. It combines both a bike lock with a piercing 100 decibel car type alarm.

Having arrived with regular cycling guest Big George, I sent him inside to grab a table while I took charge of security. I wrapped the thin security wire round our bikes and pressed the big red button to arm the alarm. Safe in the knowledge we had thwarted bike crime in Reepham I went inside to start photographing cake.

It was rather a cold day so Big George had found us a table right at the back of the café in what must have been the waiting room as it overlooked the old platform. There was a log burner in the corner giving a very warm and cosy feel. I should have been relaxed but as we were now some way from our bikes I was worried that we would not hear the alarm if the criminal fraternity of Reepham decided to pounce.

I went back outside and started to tamper with my alarm in the way that I imagined a bike thief would, at which point it did indeed emit 100 decibels of alarm which not only startled me but all the customers and staff at the cafe and nearby shop as well. I had no idea how to switch the alarm off. In hindsight, I would have needed to learn Chinese before I could have tackled the instruction leaflet but I didn't know that at the time. The deafening screech continued for an age until I finally switched it off and could sneak back in for some serious cake rating.

While enjoying some carrot cake and hoovering chat Big George stated it was the best he had ever tasted. I thought it was a good example but not stunning and slightly dry. I challenged him on his rationale and discovered that he had only eaten carrot cake once before, which had apparently been a bit rubbish. I immediately dismissed his opinion and stuck with my cake quality rating.

This highlighted how careful I would have to be with input from my cycling guests as most of the time they were clearly spouting nonsense. In future, I would only take on board their views if they agreed with mine.

*****

13

A few days later, I drove out to meet Andrew (who is notoriously hard to please) at Hard to Please House (HTPH) in the Norfolk town of Aylsham. It was his turn to host our ride and when I arrived he proudly announced that he had 'planned' a loop that would take in Reepham where he was sure there was a cafe or tearoom. This was rather disappointing news because if he had kept up to date with my blog he would have known that I went to Reepham on the last ride. It was clear that even my riding buddies were not avid blog readers.

I asked him to promise that he would read the blog in future and wanted agreement before I was happy to set off. He mumbled something, which I took to be a yes.

This time we would aim for the Reepham and Whitwell station, where I had not been and where we expected to find lots of steam train action to enjoy with our cake.

Andrew's idea of planning a route is setting off in the right general direction until we get to the edge of being lost. At this point he consults his map, points down the nearest road and we repeat the process until we get nearly lost again or get to our destination. After spending more time in the village of Foulsham than necessary, passing the church in all four directions, we found our way to Whitwell.

Despite the expected station full of steam trains, it was very light on visitors and staff. We did find the cafe building and a man in orange overalls tinkering with his gauges. He said that if there were no one in the tearoom he would make us a cup of tea. We tried the tearoom and came across a nice lady in a little office. She explained that they were only open at the weekend. She also offered to make us a cup of tea. We declined her offer but as we made our way out the man in orange overalls became very insistent in his offer of tea and we had to go through several excuses before we eventually got away and found a proper cafe. I felt that if the volunteers spent more time attracting visitors and less time drinking tea then the tearoom would be able to open 7 days a week and I could then have reviewed

My two Reepham blogs were duly posted and despite the added photographs they continued to attract only the normal numbers of reads. At the moment, the highest visits any post had was an impressive 22. I trawled the internet looking for every reference on the web of the cafes I had visited. There are a lot of sites where you can leave a review such as Yell, Google, Thompson etc. I added a short one on each with a link to the post on my blog. This took a lot of time with limited success – I gained one or two extra readers.

Visits to actual cafes were now on the back burner as I was concentrating on distribution rather than content until I overheard that Chris was planning a short ride to Wymondham with Sue (friend) whom she had persuaded to do a triathlon and who needed to do some cycling practice. I saw this as a cycle cafe rating opportunity and volunteered to come along as support crew in case of mechanical issues. My offer was accepted and I immediately raised Sue's saddle to demonstrate my bike mechanic expertise.

I knew Wymondham had a good number of tearooms that we could choose from. Once we arrived I began my hunt for today's destination by slowly cycling down the high street looking out for a good stop. Just as I was turning a corner I spotted a potential teashop opportunity. I slowed down, looked behind, pointed at the teashop and gently bumped into the raised curb. The laws of physics prove it is impossible to keep your balance when doing all these activities at once and I duly toppled over, landing softly on the edge of the road.

I was soon surrounded by a gaggle of old ladies all keen to help. Despite being completely unhurt I couldn't unclip my foot from my pedal so was trapped under my bike making my crowd of helpers think I was badly injured. When I managed to free my foot and stand up there was audible disappointment, especially from a man who had been first aid trained and seemed desperate to put me into the recovery position. As we left the scene I saw the first aid man asking the old ladies if the incident had made any of them feel faint – did anyone need to be put into the recovery position?

The Teashop was busy and cosy but a bit dark (there were several tables on the pavement outside for use on warmer days which looked a better option). The cake selection had two sponges and cheese or fruit scones. Standard fare so I awarded the appropriate effective cake selection (ECS) rating. I ordered hot chocolate and lemon sponge, Chris decaf Americano and fruit scone and Sue cappuccino and toasted tea-cake. Although toasted tea cake has the word cake in its title I consider it to be a bread and not a cake so Sue was unable to play any further part in rating the cake quality. Not the best tearoom I have visited but fine for a cycle stop.

We left the tearoom, carefully avoiding a number of old ladies lying on the pavement in the recovery position, and set off back on an uneventful ride home.

I had visited seven cafes or tearooms in the last month and with this content plus the online marketing then the site count was now over 200 after just 2 months of blogging.

Chapter 5
(Visits 207 only 49,793 to go)

With two more posts under my belt and the increased marketing I had quickly gained another 100 visits. And I'd had an idea.

It turned out to be my best yet. I decided to post a link to my blog on the Facebook page of the cafes I had visited. At first I thought this was a bit risky because if I had said anything negative about the cafe they may take offence; although this has never happened.

The Corner House café got back to me almost straight away saying how much they had enjoyed my post. They shared it with all their followers and promised they would explain the secret of their cup sizing policy if I asked on a subsequent visit. (I have but it remains a secret).

Thanks to the Facebook followers of the Corner House cafe I suddenly got 50 new hits in a couple of days. This was the first time a large number of unknown people had definitely looked at the blog. My audience was no longer just family and friends.

*****

With all this fabulous progress, it was time to arrange another ride with Barry and Helen and their tandem to show Barry just how popular my blog now was.

It was a particularly cold ride and we were all frozen when we arrived at the Courtyard café in Wymondham. I told Barry about the exciting news of real strangers reading the blog. He claimed it would only be impressive if lots of people were coming back and reading other posts about my cycling adventures. This was clearly not happening. He suggested they were probably only reading the first line, telling themselves that it was a load of old tosh and then going to YouTube to look at kittens doing amusing things.

He said to be considered an internet success I needed to get up to at least 50,000 visits. That was 49,650 more than the current 350 I had. We agreed that if I was still posting in two years' time and had had over 50,000 visits to the blog Barry would admit that I was an internet sensation, otherwise I would stop posting and delete the blog!

Just to rub it in Barry ordered a sausage roll instead of a cake. It was the start of a continuing trend and his way of further undermining my work. I decided to rise above it but made it clear that he would be playing no further part in any cake-related rating this day. He seemed surprisingly unbothered by his exclusion as the rest of us got down to some serious cake tasting.

Christmas would soon be upon us but I still had time to squeeze in two last café cycle reviews.

The first was from HTPH in Aylsham. As always when Andrew oversees 'planning' then the route, ride distance, destination, etc. aren't confirmed until just after they have happened. I was therefore surprised when he suggested we went to Holt and then claimed he had done some Holt café-based research on his laptop. I was impressed until it materialised that the research had only confirmed that there were, in fact, cafes in Holt, a fact I was already aware of. Unsurprisingly he had not managed to decide which one to visit so I picked Horatios.

It was a glorious crisp December morning only spoiled by Andrew's rant about the number of out of date cafe reviews he had come across during his research, blaming this on his failure to pick an actual cafe venue.

"Who is responsible for keeping these things up to date on the internet?" he ranted at me. I had to admit I didn't know and this somehow led on to a moan about what will happen when the web cloud thing fills up due to irresponsible people storing their rubbish photos, that they would never look at again, in the virtual world. We arrived at Horatios and I asked Andrew to take the requisite post photo of me outside. He took several - further clogging up the web cloud thing!

I was glad to see that Horatios had an outside eating area but it was squeezed on to a very narrow pavement and only seemed suitable for use by extremely thin people so we went inside where I was immediately struck by the enormous number of tempting cakes available. They obviously like their cake in Holt, which probably explains why the "very thin people only" outdoor seating area was empty.

*****

I was going to have one final ride this year. But my cycling guest Big George, had to get back in time to prepare for the Big George Family Annual Christmas drinks party. Mrs Big George was at work and didn't know he was sneaking out to play with me instead of doing his pre-party chores. Mrs Big George doesn't approve of me distracting her husband away from his housework duties on his day off so it was a hush-hush operation and a short ride.

As we were in a hurry we set off far too fast and got to our destination, the imaginatively named 'The Coffee Shop' in Wymondham, gasping for breath.

The cake selection was rather scone rich so we had scones followed by a pleasant time discussing housework matters of the day until Big George suddenly confessed that he never actually read the blog although he was happy to be involved. Unlike Barry I still hoped to break him one day as at least he was still ordering cake (although as we will find this did not last).

As we talked we completely lost track of time. Big George suddenly looked at his watch and realised it was now too late for him to make the Christmas canapés for which he had become famous. We spent the way home coming up with excuses for him to tell Mrs Big George as to why there would be no canapés at the party. The best we could think of was that when his back was turned the dog ate them. It was only when I arrived at the drinks party that evening I remembered they didn't have a dog and we had been rumbled.

Worse still, Mrs Big George told me she didn't let Big George work only four days a week just so he could go out on bike rides with me and he was therefore grounded.

As Christmas approached I took stock of the first two and a half months. I was now up to nearly 400 blog visits, which was over five a day. At the current rate, it would only take 26 years (slightly less if you include leap years) to hit the 50,000 target so I still had a bit of work to do.

I realised that going on local rides to nearby cafes was already getting a bit dull so needed to up my game with some rather more dramatic ideas. Fortunately one was just around the corner.

Chapter 6
(Visits 398 only 49,602 to go)

After a quiet Christmas, we had arrived at Boxing Day for the traditional meet up with Duncan (brother) and his Family for traditional gift exchange. Up to now my family had been a mixture of both apathetic and supportive towards the blog. I demanded that Chris and son George read each post as soon as it went live and would stand over them until they complied. They made the right encouraging noises and despite the potential embarrassment, George was even prepared to share the odd post with his Facebook friends. Peter (student son) still avoided any blog discussion and preferred to pretend it didn't exist.

Chris seemed to enjoy finding the spelling and grammar mistakes more than the actual content but I always appreciated her feedback and made the corrections she demanded. My Mother also told me she liked the posts but she was clueless on how Facebook worked so was unable to share the posts with her Facebook friends.

After presents had been handed out and Christmas was complete for another year I steered us back to the key topic of the day and once again started to discuss the Norfolk Café Cycle Tour blog, my mission to become an internet sensation. I was hoping to get Duncan and his sons sucked in as regular readers to help up the post count.

Before I had a chance to expand on any of my adventures Duncan just said 'who would want to read about your bike rides and what cake you have eaten? Haven't you got anything better to do with your time?' He then quoted from a book he was reading saying that people who write blogs, post on Facebook, tweet etc. were just trying to massage their tiny egos.

This was not the support I was after. "This is not about my ego" I said, taking the moral high ground, "but my way of putting something back into the community to encourage people to get out on their bikes and help fight the obesity epidemic in this country".

"Where does encouraging people to eat cake fit in with your national weight loss agenda?" he asked. "Fact", I said, (always a good opening when you are about to make up your own data), "you burn 15-20 times the calories of a cake on a bike ride." "Rubbish, it is probably calorie neutral at best" he scoffed.

It was clear that neither of us had the necessary information to support our arguments although we continued to make a lot of "facts" up for the next half hour. By now the rest of the family had drifted off to watch Christmas celebrity dancing in the jungle so I abandoned any attempt to make new converts for the day.

Once I was home again I typed 'calories per cake' into Google. The answer that best supported my argument suggested that an average hot chocolate and cake is about 400 calories. Further searches revealed that you burn approximately 600 calories for every ten miles you cycle (depending on speed, weight etc.) I did the maths which showed that on a 20-mile bike ride you could safely have three café and cake stops without putting on any weight. It seemed extremely unlikely even to me but that's what the internet said so it must be true.

This gave me an idea: I would attempt to set a world record for the most cafes visited on a calorie neutral bike ride. Such an event was sure not only to give the blog lots of extra publicity but had the added bonus of proving to Duncan that I was embarked on a noble endeavour to tackle the obesity epidemic (even if it was really just about my ego).

So now I had a full three-point café cycle plan to tackle
1. Set a world record for most cafes visited on a calorie neutral bicycle ride
2. Become an internet sensation by achieving 50,000 visits to my blog within two years

3. Get Duncan and Barry to admit they were wrong

As New Year approached I was looking forward to an exciting year, which it proved to be but not in the way I was expecting, when, a couple of months later, I woke up in intensive care after a near death experience (NDE).

Chapter 7
(Visits 407 only 49,593 to go)

With my three-point plan in place there was no time to be lost as Chris and I set off to Hard to Please House to join up with Andrew for the first ride of the year. It was a very windy day so he had planned a shortish ride to his favourite café at Heydon village. As we were blown about trying to get the bikes out of the car we all agreed that a short ride was a good call.

I didn't want to postpone the ride as I had been looking forward to listening to Andrew's Christmas and New Year rants and he didn't disappoint. His main focus concentrated on the pointlessness of being forced to give and receive presents on a particular day and the role of Santa in the sorry affair.

Although it was very windy it was also rather mild but Chris had dressed for an Artic expedition. This meant that every few minutes she removed an item and handed it to me to carry (headband, inner gloves, outer gloves, scarf etc.) as apparently, carrying her excess clothing was my job. I did my best as I stuffed them into every available pocket, increasing my drag coefficient with every item.

As we rounded the final corner we spotted a fellow cyclist who had stopped and was photographing the hedge. He had the guilty look of a man caught in the act of doing something very naughty. I can only think he must have stopped for an emergency cycling comfort break and that he likes to take a photo of where he had been (literally). Maybe he had a cycle comfort break rating blog and I made a note to check it out (he hasn't).

The cakes at Heydon tea shop were excellent but Andrew wanted to big everything up as he likes this café above all others. It is one of the best but I had to bring some sense to his insistence that everything be rated 10 out of 10 as he did appear a touch biased and not his normal notoriously hard to please self.

After I had spent some time normalising the ratings from Andrew's input we were blown back to Aylsham before returning home where I posted for the first time that year although the blog post didn't seem to generate much interest. During the ride, I had been distracted not only by Andrew's constant ranting but thinking about the calorie neutral cycling gauntlet that Duncan had thrown down. Once home I logged straight on to the Guinness Book of Records website. I explained my record as follows:

I'm a keen cyclist and cafe/tearoom visitor. I have recently been trying to visit as many cafes on my bike as I can. I would therefore like to set a record of visiting the most cafes/tearooms on a single bike ride. However, I feel any visit needs to include a hot drink and piece of cake. Therefore, the rule on this ride is that the next café/tearoom cannot be visited until all the calories from the last cafe/tearoom have been burnt thus making the ride calorie neutral. I calculate an average cake and hot chocolate is 400 calories so these must be cycled off before the next cafe stop. I reckon a good cyclist would do this in about half an hour over about 9-10 miles. I think a world record target of 20 cafes on a single ride would be challenging as that would involve about 200 miles cycling fast, eating 20 bits of cake plus 20 hot drinks, planning the optimum route, finding cafes open at right times etc.

I will measure it with a pulse/calorie counter showing 400 calories have been burnt before each cafe stop, photo evidence at each cafe of calories burnt and sign off from cafe that I ate the cake and drank the drink.

I'm doing this as I want to promote cycling as I'm very keen to encourage people to get out on their bikes to help solve the obesity epidemic in this country.

Later research showed that my calorie facts were wrong but I was confident that with the help of the Guinness world record (GWR) research team we would get the right numbers. GWR said it would take them about 12 weeks to research and validate any new record before they authorise it. I sat back in my chair knowing I had plenty of time before real planning would need to start.

I was going to have to find a lot more cafes with a good spread of opening times so when Barry and Helen and their Tandem suggested a ride to the Hill Top Café in Rackheath I was extra keen as I noticed it opened at 6:30 in the morning.

I was suspicious as to why Barry had suddenly suggested we go on a ride to a café. Up to now he had always disapproved of cafes and tearooms and wanted to cycle to the pub so clearly something was up. I discovered he had found another café reviewing website which also featured cafes in the Norwich area as well as ones in London. This was the Fry Up Inspector although his modus operandi was quite different as there was no cycling involved and he was only interested in fried breakfast quality. He had been going a lot longer than me and clearly had a different market but I was rather jealous that he had had huge numbers of visits to his blog, which made my few hundred look a bit pathetic even if I hadn't yet been going three months.

As we prepared to leave I realised the weather looked distinctly dodgy until the skies cleared and all looked set fair for a lovely cycle. But by the time we had got to the meeting point the skies had re-darkened, it had started to drizzle and the further we rode the heavier the rain got.

On arrival at the Hill Top café we dripped our way inside, hanging our wet gear across several tables.

The Hilltop cafe is only small but the staff seemed very friendly despite us turning their indoor seating area into a Chinese laundry. The sign outside had said breakfast, lunch and home-made cakes. But sadly, the only home-made cakes were Norfolk shortbread (a biscuit), apple and date crumble (a dessert) and sausage roll (a savoury snack) so strictly speaking no home-made cakes. Worse still, there was no mention of hot chocolate on the menu. Talking to the waitress it became apparent that the café was aimed more at the early morning commuter in search of a fried breakfast than the cake eater. She said she could do me a hot chocolate and as the apple and date crumble looked a bit like flapjack (which counts as a cake) I decided enough was in place for ratings and reviewing to happen.

After I ordered my hot chocolate and 'flapjack' Chris, Barry and Helen all ordered a mug of filter coffee and then went for the full English breakfast as their cake option.

A full English breakfast is not cake. I had no option but to exclude them from playing any further part in rating the Hilltop Cafe. I knew that Barry had deliberately picked the café based on the Fry Up Inspector's recommendation, knowing that it would not suit my needs. Magnanimously, I decided not to rise to the bait and changed the subject back to who had got wettest.

As Chris was able to wring gallons of water out of her socks we didn't even need Arthur Ellis's dip-stick to declare the winner. For some reason the news of her victory did not cheer her up as she continued to mutter about being cold and wet and stupid blogs. When I wrote up the post I decided to call our wet ride aqua biking, which proved to be a good idea although I didn't yet know it. I exchanged messages with the Fry Up Inspector and we agreed to put links to each other's blogs on our sites.

Chapter 8
(Visits 742 only 49,258 to go)

I didn't know how long it would be before bad weather made café cycling impossible. I therefore decided to cram in as many rides as I could. With each blog averaging about 30 hits I calculated I would only have to do another 1600 café cycle ride posts to reach the 50,000 target. I suspected that there were not another 1600 cafes within cycling distance but I wasn't looking for problems just solutions.

The first ride was with Big George to one of his favourite cafes, Rosy Lee's tearoom in Loddon. You may have already noticed that cycling with Big George normally comes with a last minute critical deadline and this ride was no exception. Just before we set of he explained that, to help Big George Jnr's A level studies Mrs Big George had decided a new carpet, desk and desk lamp would encourage the imminent demands of revision. (We had had the same thoughts for our son and had returned his floordrobe to carpet to try and improve his revision environment. No signs that it made a difference but we did find a lot of missing cutlery and plates).

Whilst they were in the carpet shop a last-minute cancellation had made a carpet-fitting slot available for 1 o'clock today. Big George claimed he had tried to rearrange but with Mrs Big George standing beside him the words 'but I've agreed to go cycling on Friday' somehow came out as 'that's fine'. We therefore had to be back in time to avoid putting Big George Jnr's university education in jeopardy.

With the deadline in place we rode at pace down to Loddon. Big George refused to engage in any conversation on his domestic chores as apparently, I had been showing a lack of discretion in what I had been posting about. Reporting his views on cooking and cleaning in the blog was ruining his hard man image. I couldn't be certain but I did get the impression he was very pleased with his newly purchased purple Dyson's cleaning power and its smooth ball action.

Once at Rosy Lee's Tearoom we chose to go inside rather than make use of either of the seats in the outdoor continental style pavement seating area. Rosy Lee's Tearoom is small but very popular and there have been times in the past when we haven't managed to get a seat. Today we came 'off Peak' and opted for the table by the counter and cakes.

Big George and I both fancied the date and walnut cake, which was a shame as I prefer different cakes to be tried - to get a more rounded cake taste quality (CTQ) score. I knew that Big George often panics when ordering his refreshments so I easily managed to trick him into having a cheese scone.

After our very pleasant stop we still had plenty of time to get Big George back to make his carpet fitter appointment and thus guarantee his son a university education. We set off at a steady pace confident nothing could go wrong. But when Big George took a call from the carpet fitter, he discovered that he was coming early! The race was now on, I knew I didn't want to get into Mrs Big George's bad books again, so shot off as fast as I could go. Big George kept up with me to start with but soon started to flag. 'Come on' I shouted, 'we must save your son's university education'. When he caught up he was red in the face, out of breath and looking ready to collapse. He suggested that we slow down and that he could always concentrate on his other son's education instead. I agreed that sounded like a better plan and we continued home at a more leisurely pace discussing how expensive and overrated university is anyway.

I later discovered that the carpet fitter had got lost and Big George made it home in time meaning I avoided another black mark in Mrs Big George's naughty boys' book.

*****

There was no time for rest and a couple of days later I was off again, this time with Chris. I had foolishly entered an Ironman Triathlon in the following summer so was in full training mode and thought it would be good to do a session on my indoor bike trainer first before the ride proper out to The Mill Cafe Bar and Restaurant at Yaxham.

Things didn't start well with a puncture after 40 mins. Not, as you might imagine, out on the wet and muddy roads but while I was on the indoor bike. The manufacturers do claim that it is the most realistic ride you can have and as I do get a lot of punctures then maybe this is a design feature.

It was a difficult day to judge the day's temperature and neither of us were confident we had got our clothing layers right. After a couple of miles, I checked my feet-ometer and realised I had lost the feeling in my toes. I knew I should have double socked! We stopped to add extra clothing layers and then it was fast pedalling, head down into the wind to try and warm up on the way to Yaxham.

The Mill Cafe Bar and Restaurant is very friendly and we had a nice chat with Hugo the owner. He asked how we had heard of them so I proudly told him about my blog. He trumped my potential blog review of his cafe (readership of 30 per post) by telling me they had been reviewed in the local paper (EDP) yesterday (readership about 59,493). At first I was disappointed but I did the maths and realised that if my blog readership continues to grow at its current rate then I will have more readers than the EDP in about 37 years' time. Sadly, the Mill Cafe Bar and Restaurant closed a year later with my review still nearly 59,000 behind.

But it did give me an idea and I made a note to try and get my blog in the EDP when my café coverage had grown and I could try and leverage their 59,493 readers.

After we had been warmed by our drinks and food we were about to leave when Hugo came over to explain that they were doing some publicity shots of their restaurant food and if we didn't mind eating photographed food then we could have it or it would go to waste. Although we were both full from our cake we took him up on his kind offer as this really did sound like such a thing as a free lunch.

Despite Hugo's concerns, the photographed venison burger was excellent and had clearly not been adversely affected by the number of pictures that had been taken of it.

According to my feet-ometer the temperature had warmed up and we now had the wind behind for the ride back. Progress was slow as I had two more punctures but, as my mother always tells me, 'bad things come in threes' so I should have been clear of punctures for a bit. (As it turned out she was wrong, and I wasn't).

*****

It was time to try a different approach to generate some new readers. I had been on a few organised group cycle rides, which are known as sportives.

My idea was to have Norfolk Café Cycle tour sportives where I would organise group rides to my favourite venues. To start with I would just invite my cycling friends but I was confident that once word got out people would be begging to be allowed to join the rides. (They haven't).

The benefits for me of a Norfolk Café Cycle Tour sportive would be
1. An excuse to go back to best cafes,
2. The chance to write a different style of post
3. To encourage each participant to read the blog

I choose the destination based on its rating, how far we wanted to go and the wind direction. The Cafe at Brooke ticked all the sportive cafe selection boxes, so I arranged a 26-mile route stopping there.

Five riders had signed up for the first event. The large number of participants meant I had to delay the start by 5 minutes while general faffing about occurred but the ride eventually got under way as a blur of hi-viz yellow hurtled out of Norwich.

Once at Brooke we found our way to the café. We ordered our drinks and cakes and I gathered the scores for the first ever group marking which went a lot smoother than expected and much more smoothly than I was to encounter on future Norfolk Café Tour sportives.

It was here I started my next quest, this time on the knotty subject of scone serving temperature. I had been particularly pleased to be asked if I wanted hot or cold blueberry scone. I strongly believe that a fruit scone should be cold and a cheese scone warm for the optimum scone consumption temperature (OSCT). I have regularly had a warm fruit scone foisted on me in the past which is not only an unnecessary waste of energy but inevitably results in a low cake taste quality (CTQ) rating as it crumbles in my mits. To help everyone remember what to do I made up a rhyme "cheese scone hot, fruit scone not" which I was rather pleased with and vowed to make sure this practice was adopted by all cafes in future. More data and spreadsheets were quickly set up.

After the ride feedback was collected and processed with the first Norfolk Cafe Cycle Tour Sportive being declared a success (by me).

I posted my first sportive post and waited for it to quickly shoot up my post views league table. To my disappointment, it became my lowest read post to date with only a handful of hits in the first few days and none by the people who had come with me. This was a blow - what I had been sure was a winning idea had proved another flop.

*****

While trying to think up some new ways to attract followers I saw that the Guinness World Record people had got back to me and I expectantly opened the e-mail to see what I needed to do next. They had said that I would not hear back from them for about 12 weeks', giving the Guinness World Records experts time to review my record breaking bid and set the standard I needed to achieve. So, I was surprised that it had been nearer 12 days when they had sent me their decision.

The opening started well as they said *"We are always **delighted** when we hear from people who want to break a record and were **excited** to read your application."* Not only were they delighted to hear from me but my application had got them excited.

But then the bomb shell. *"Unfortunately, after **thoroughly** reviewing your application with members of our research team, we are afraid to say that we're unable to accept your proposal as a Guinness World Records title."* Clearly their delight and excitement had quickly worn off.

Their explanation continued, stating that *"Every record verified by Guinness World Records must be measurable by a single superlative, verifiable, standardisable, breakable and also present an element of skill. Also, no gluttony records are allowed."*

To be fair the record does fail against most of their criteria even if standardisable isn't a proper word, although I was hoping they could make an exception for such a marvellous idea that had initially caused so much delight and excitement in the Guinness World Records offices.

They did try to raise my spirits by pointing out that *"Only a handful of new records categories are accepted every year"* but finished by washing their hands of me altogether with a P.S of *"If you choose to proceed, then this will be of your own volition and at your own risk. Guinness World Records will not monitor, measure or verify this activity."*

I decided this would not be the end of my world record ambitions and that I would undertake my own research by having a trial run of five cafes to see what was practical. Based on that I would set a Norfolk Cafe Cycle Tour verified world record target and pencilled in a date in September for my attempt. When I succeeded, I would make my own World Record certificate using my colouring set.

Chapter 9
(Visits 1024 only 48,976 to go)

It was clear that concentrating my efforts predominantly in Norfolk wasn't attracting the necessary volume of interested café, cake and cycling fans. It was time to think about going international. Big George had recently told me he had always wanted to cycle from London to Paris. History tells us that Big George's plans never materialise but I arranged to meet up for a ride to discuss it further and see how his research was coming along.

As always something had cropped up so he could only do a short trip. I worked out the shortest café ride we could do was a third of a mile to Stephanie's Coffee House just down the road from my house. We both agreed that was a bit too short so we decided on a quick 20-mile loop before calling in to rate Stephanie's Coffee House in advance of a very short ride home.

It was a cold and frosty January morning. Once we got out into the countryside the roads were far icier than we had realised. After a few back-wheel skids, we both became very tentative and rode accordingly. This also cut down the conversation as we had to concentrate on not falling off. With the slow pace, and a puncture thrown in, we arrived at Stephanie's Coffee House much later than expected.

The café's main competition is from the nearby Waitrose, which now hands out free hot drinks to anyone in need of them, like a sort of coffee-based soup kitchen for the middle classes. However, Stephanie's provided a far more relaxed location for an important planning meeting.

We were rather cold so pleased to see the seat by the radiator was free. With my hot chocolate, I ordered a raspberry and something (couldn't remember what) flapjack.

Big George went for cappuccino and a pain aux raisin. The pain aux raisin is clearly a leavened butter pastry and not a cake so he could not take part in any cake quality rating. It had to be based on the raspberry and something flapjack alone.

This was the first meeting of our working group to plan Big George's proposed London to Paris cycle ride (which probably explained why Big George selected a pain aux raisin instead of a cake). As I predicted Big George's research was still in the conceptual phase but the meeting went well with no decisions made other than to have another meeting on our next ride. It brought back pre-retirement memories of how meetings in Big Business used to be, except without the bikes. I knew that if the ride was ever to happen I would have to take over - meaning I could make the whole expedition far more cake-based thus attracting an international audience to the blog.

On leaving Stephanie's Coffee house I discovered I had had another puncture but at least it was only a very short walk to wheel it home (a third of a mile to be precise).

When I got home, Chris met me at the door with some exciting news. One of her friends was due to meet a new male friend in North Walsham so had asked if anyone could recommend a cafe in the area where they could meet. Unfortunately, this was a part of Norfolk that I had not yet managed to explore but as luck would have it I was due to meet up for a ride with Andrew at HTPH, which is not too far from North Walsham. I asked him to research the cafe we should go to. On arrival, he told me he had done thorough research and had picked the aptly named Liaison cafe as it had had a good review for fried eggs. His logic was that if you can fry an egg you can bake a cake, which seemed fair enough, so we set off.

As our mission began it started to rain, then sleet and snow, the roads started to flood and we were soon freezing. Andrew wasn't sure if he was enjoying himself and claimed he could no longer feel his fingers. To keep him motivated I reminded him that nobody ever said cafe cycle rating was going to be easy. Surprisingly this didn't seem to help so I agreed we could take a short cut.

On arrival at the café I went to review the cakes while Andrew dealt with drinks and received the devastating news that the coffee machine was being repaired. Although this didn't impact on my hot chocolate he had to make do with a mug of tea, not good news for someone who is notoriously hard to please.

At Liaison cafe, there is a choice of a formal or comfy indoor seating area. We went for the comfy area where, as well as sofas there was a random pole going from floor to ceiling. I imagined that this was to attract the passing fireman or pole dancer trade. There didn't appear to be any in today so we sat in the sofas and got on with rating our cakes and hot drinks.

Although Liaisons cafe had a reasonable rating I didn't think it was outstanding enough to be recommended to Chris's friend. I did check she was not a pole dancer or a fireman. Unsurprisingly she wasn't so I had to chalk up my first café commission as a fail.

*****

With visitor numbers starting to show a tiny but steady increase I thought it was time to implement my latest genius idea. I would introduce a new useful routes facility. I worked out how to convert each ride's route to Google maps and then embed it at the bottom of each post. Now any keen cyclists could start to use my blog as a library of routes even if they did all start from outside my house. I worried that my driveway would get blocked as cyclists turned up to set off on their chosen ride although surprisingly to date this has not been the case.

I wanted to draw attention to this new feature so needed a new ride where I could add the map and point my readers to the useful route facility on the blog. I persuaded Chris that a nice ride in the cold and wet down to the Spoon Cake Cafe in Loddon would be a lovely way to spend a winter's morning. The ride to Loddon also turned out to be into the wind and ended with yet another puncture so, although not talking, we were pleased to get to the Spoon Cake Café.

The cakes and drinks were both very good with the Spoon Café rated highly - however I did have one concern. The cafe had moved away from the standard system of giving each table its own number. Instead they had adopted a system based on the name of a herb. We chose the Thyme table.

On closer inspection, it became clear all was not well in the herb-based table identification system department. To go with Thyme there were the predictable Parsley, Sage and Rosemary tables leaving three further tables to be allocated a herb-based name. The next one I looked at was Basil, another good herb choice I thought but then we got to table Lavender. Although not strictly a herb, more of a fragrant flower, Lavender can be used in cooking so I thought they just about got away with it. But what of the last table, to my horror it had a completely off piste label of Nutmeg. Nutmeg is clearly not a herb or even a fragrant plant but a spice and I could see no place for it in any self-respecting herb based table identification system.

I explained to Chris what was disturbing me but she couldn't understand why it was such a big deal. I tried to elaborate with a simple scenario. What would happen if a school child came into the cafe with their parent for a post-school treat. Little Johnny might think to themselves, 'oh look, there appears to be a herb based table identification system in operation, I shall take this opportunity to learn my herbs'. Back at school when the teacher asks if anyone can name a herb, little Jonny would put up his hand and say nutmeg. The rest of the class will fall about laughing at him and he would be ridiculed for the rest of his school days before dropping out of school and ending up a homeless drug addict in the Loddon area, always to be known as Nutmeg. I felt my point had been well and truly proved as Chris had no response to this, possibly as she had long since glazed over.

Interestingly, when I returned to the café a few months later the herb- based table identification was no longer in operation and I suspect the number of homeless drug addicts in the Loddon area had also fallen.

*****

As we were now in the midst of winter there were fewer cycling opportunities, leaving plenty of time to analyse the blog stats. In the early days, I could identify by name who each person who had read a post was but after some rides strange things were happening count wise.

The first time this happened was after a very uneventful ride to the Tudor Bake House and coffee shop in Long Stratton. The Tudor Bake House and coffee shop was a pleasant enough stop though there was absolutely nothing Tudor about it, no Tudor architecture, no mock Tudor beams and no dead Tudor kings buried in the car park.

I digress, as the style of architecture was not the key mystery but for some reason this post, which was not one of my best, suddenly got lots of visits and was soon my most read review. In fact, over the next few weeks it became the first post with over 200 visits which was 10 times more than most of the others but I had no idea why. Then suddenly, no hits at all. This phenomenon continued to crop up from time to time on particular posts, sometimes ones that had not been looked at for several months. I never worked out the cause, but I hoped it was because someone had come across it and shared it with their friends. But it didn't really matter - it was getting me closer to becoming an Internet sensation and that's all that really mattered.

Shortly after this the same thing happened with my post to the Hilltop café. Over the next year, it consistently got over 50 views a month and was my first post to 500. I had called the post Aqua biking and discovered that this was in fact a recognised thing used mainly for injury rehab when people cycle on a fixed bike in a swimming pool. It was also a fitness fad used by overweight Americans. I assumed that people must have been coming across my post when they were in fact looking for a fitness machine. I did feel guilty about the possibility that I was probably encouraging already fat Americans to eat more cake. But after a year there were no more visits to this post and as Aqua biking still exists then this couldn't have been the case. Unless the word had gone around America that eating cake underwater made it go a bit mushy so people stopped checking out my post.

New rides and reviews started to become harder to organise as cycling guests didn't seem keen to go out when it was cold, wet and windy. I had to come up with alternative approaches to get people to come along as they were needed to review the Guest Hot Drink Quality (GHDQ). I managed to persuade Big George to join me with a plan to cycle to Brandon Country Park Café (wind behind) and then catch the train back.

Things started badly when Big George arrived, as there was an even frostier atmosphere than usual. I assumed that it was because I had failed to notice the new aerobars on his bike, a bit like failing to spot a lady's new hairdo, but once he had pointed them out there was clearly still something else bothering him.

It transpired that Chris had been to a parent evening at our son's school. The session was an attempt to teach parents how to get their teenage child do the necessary revision for their A 'levels (a fairly fruitless exercise). She had been taken in by the presentation and was now convinced it was possible to encourage your child to do some work rather than waste their time looking at pointless blogs and Facebook pages. She had diligently written up the notes to e-mail to me and our sons (like many modern families, despite living in the same house and often being in the same room, we find email and text the most effective way to communicate).

This system had, however, been her downfall as she had mistakenly sent the email to Big George instead of Son George. Big George had taken this as an unsolicited and patronising slur on both his parenting skills and criticism of his son's revising ability. Apparently, family honour was now at stake. I smoothed things over by agreeing to buy his cake and we spent the rest of the ride discussing the pros and cons of a colour-coded revision timetable system.

It turned out to be a wasted visit: the café was disappointing and the post attracted very few visits.

*****

I had now achieved just over 1,500 visits in five months so I forecast it would take only 14 more years to hit Barry's target but I only had another 19 months. I didn't want this to be a jail sentence so I felt action was needed to speed things up: time for a new three-point plan.

1. Keep doing plenty of café reviews and always post on the café's Facebook page
2. Undertake London to Paris café cycle ride with Big George to spread the word to the capital and le continent
3. Start the publicity for my calorie neutral bike ride world record.

With renewed vigour, I vowed to ramp things up.

As we entered March I was getting two or three rides in a week and with one of my Sportives thrown in for good measure it was clear part one of my plan was up and running. I felt it was time to catch up with Barry to bring him up to date. We would obviously throw in a café review for good measure but where to go?

I had decided it was high time I went to what most people would consider the benchmark for cafes: A National Trust property. I had chosen Muddy Boots cafe at Blickling Hall, which had been recommended to me. The strap line for the cafe is: "you'll always find good coffee and a warm welcome here". Please note the use of the word "always".

As we live on opposite sides of Norwich we had arranged to meet up halfway between our houses for the official start of the route. I was joined by Chris and Barry would be bringing Helen and their tandem. We arrived promptly at the start point but there was no sign of Barry or Helen or their tandem so I immediately suspected sabotage. Barry must have guessed that having a National Trust tearoom on my blog was likely to quickly go viral and I would hit my target in record time, and he was now running scared. While I was coming up with my conspiracy theory Chris was doing some texting, which revealed that their tandem had punctured and they would be late. We spent a happy 45 minutes counting clouds, twiddling thumbs and watching grass grow.

I foolishly felt very smug as after all my recent punctures I had just purchased new 'bomb proof' tyres and I could happily mock Barry for his tyre choices all the way to Blickling. When we eventually set off I discovered I had fallen foul of some excellent tyre company marketing. The new tyres may well have been 'bomb proof', but they certainly were not puncture proof as I got both a front and back wheel puncture within the first few miles.

Due to all the delays, I had to break the news that we would not be having the planned pub stop they had requested and which I had promised after we had finished "faffing" around in a tearoom. This did not go down well as apparently a beer stop is a must for tandem cyclists and there was much whingeing and mumbling. I suggested that Barry could always start a cycle pub review blog and invite me along instead.

There was a tense atmosphere during the rest of the way to Muddy Boots tearoom so to break the ice I thought I would cheer Barry up by telling him the latest blog news: that I was now likely to hit his 50,000-visitor target in 14 years, which although not quite on plan was a vast improvement on my previous update. Surprisingly he wasn't very impressed although he did admit that the sooner I hit the target the better so we could talk about something other than cake quality on a bike ride and get back to drinking beer.

There was little more chatter until we pulled into the busy Blickling Hall National Trust car park, the location of the Muddy Boots café. On arrival, I saw that the car park was full of National Trust type people. Worried that the National Trust type people would have scoffed all the cake we rushed towards the tearoom.

We needn't have bothered as it transpired that the Muddy Boots café was shut

I did, of course, write to the National Trust to complain about the inaccurate website and insist that their café strap line be changed. How about *"when we can be bothered to open you will find potentially good coffee (subject to a GHDQ review) and a warm welcome here"*. I am still waiting for a reply.

I ignored suggestions from Barry and Helen and their tandem that we could go to the pub instead and insisted we head straight to nearby Aylsham to find a café to review. Which we did and quickly came across the Food Lovers Café Deli.

I had hot chocolate and orange and carrot cake. Chris had skinny mocha and soup (which is not cake). Barry and Helen and their tandem were still sulking about the lack of beer so just had soup and no drinks. I made it clear they would therefore play no further part in cycle cafe reviewing of the Food Lovers Café Deli, which rather undermined their role as guest reviewers although they appeared surprisingly unbothered.

The Food Lovers Café Deli was a good cycle stop but it had not been a very successful ride and Barry was now more convinced than ever that café cycle reviewing was a complete waste of time and the sooner we got back to cycling to the pub the better.

Worse still, on the return journey I got my 3rd puncture so decided the 'bomb proof' tyres needed to go although to date I have found no way of destroying them as they are indeed bomb proof.

I had really got into the swing of how this café cycle blogging worked and could bang out a post within a couple of hours of finishing a ride, subject to the need for an afternoon kip. I was confident things were getting on track. Little did I know that when I set off on my next ride it would very nearly be my last one ever.

Chapter 10
(Visits 2356 only 47,644 to go)

When I'm not cycling, or eating cake I love running. I had arranged a weekend break to Barcelona and as luck would have it, the date we were there was when Barcelona were having their marathon. It was too good an opportunity to miss so I decided to enter it. Chris said it was weird just how often I discover there is a running race or triathlon happening at our holiday destination at exactly the time we are there.

The race, and weekend, went well but café cycle blogs don't get extra visitors from running races so although my legs were rather tired I was keen to get out on another ride.

I had chosen to cycle to the interestingly named Hen House Café with Chris as my cycling guest.

We found the café at the end of a shingle path that led up to a big hall. While locking our bikes I noticed that there was not only a normal outdoor seating area but also one that was shed-based. Once we had bought our cakes and drinks we selected a shed to sit in.

I found the shed based seating area a master-stroke as there is nothing better than pottering about in a shed. I settled down ready to spend the afternoon tinkering but there were too many soft furnishings and wall decorations and not enough useless mechanical things to fiddle with. I would rather have fewer cushions and more cogs. I think a trick had been missed here but the shed and furnishing fusion seemed to go down better with Chris who was happily flickering through a magazine about chocolate and curtains. She would have happily stayed all afternoon but with nothing mechanical needing my attention we finished our drinks and cakes and headed home.

Back on the bikes I felt a bit of tummy ache coming on, which I can assure you had nothing to do with the excellent refreshments we had just had. I thought no more of it but throughout the evening I had a continuing twinge in my stomach. As it got worse I opted to go to bed early hoping it would have passed overnight.

By the next morning, the pain was quite bad and I had to cancel a ride with Big George. Even the thought of rightfully being the butt of his jokes for calling off couldn't get me out of bed.

After another painful night it was clear that the duathlon I had entered the next day was not going to be happening either so Chris took charge by phoning the NHS helpline. They suggested I went to the local hospital walk in centre.

When we arrived, there was a bit of a queue but I was feeling too uncomfortable sitting down so I decided to lay on the floor. This proved to be a good trick as hospitals and GP surgeries don't seem very keen on having patients flaked out groaning in their waiting areas so I was hurried in to see the doctor. (Feel free to use this top tip next time you have to wait for hours in the doctor's surgery).

As expected the nice lady doctor checked my vital signs (blood pressure, temperature etc.) and told me to keep taking the tablets and it should all be better in a day or so. She wasn't sure what the problem was as it could have been one of many things but if it did get worse she teed up a fast path into A&E so I didn't have to queue up again and litter their waiting room floor with my body. It is a similar system to the one they use for rich people on the busy rides at Disneyland, but free to people in a lot of pain.

I was due to go on a cycling holiday in Nice with Andrew (who is notoriously hard to please) a couple of weeks later. As I lay at home waiting to get better I was feeling glad that this trip would still be able to go ahead as I expected to be back on the bike in a couple of days' time. I was just starting to doze off whilst thinking about bicycles, café and cake when, like John Hurt in the film Alien, boom! I got hit with a wave of intense pain although fortunately no creatures burst out of my tummy.

Chris came to see what was wrong and decided to put operation fast pass A&E into action. The paramedics turned up within a few minutes and whisked me away in an ambulance.

This was not the first time I had been whisked away in an ambulance clutching my stomach. Twelve years earlier my appendix had burst and I had ended up rolling round outside a motorway service station, which was my first hospital near death experience but that is another story.

Once on board I was strapped in and offered gas and air which I gratefully accepted. I was still conscious enough to be disappointed that the siren and flashing blue light had not been put on and worried that they clearly didn't think my condition was serious enough.

Once in hospital things became a bit of a blur. After I was checked in and seen by a doctor in A&E I was sent to a ward. At this stage, they were not exactly sure what the cause of the pain was. I was showing all the symptoms of kidney stones but the most likely cause seemed to be a twisted bowel caused by my intestine being caught on my appendix scar from the emergency operation twelve years earlier.

I had no concept of time as I dozed in and out of sleep. I awoke to find that I was being wheeled off to the operating theatre. As the porters came and put me on their special trolley I thought it was Saturday evening but it was now Sunday afternoon and I was still moaning.

*****

I opened my eyes and saw Chris sitting by my bed. She started to explain what had happened to me.

Apparently it was now Tuesday and this wasn't the first time I had come around but I couldn't remember any of the previous occasions.

From what Chris and the doctors told me I worked out that the actual operation had gone fine and 12cm of my intestine had been removed. They had cut me along my old appendix scar and I was being held together by metal staples and sticking tape.

Over the next few days I discovered that during the operation my acid levels had been very high and I had gone into septic shock, causing my organs to try to shut down. I was put on a ventilator to help me breathe as my heart could no longer keep up and they had to keep me sedated.

A few weeks later I found out I was given only a 50/50 chance of waking up at all, and that a new trial drug had helped stabilise my organs.

Now I was back in the land of the living I decided it was time to start getting better as I didn't know how long it would be before I could get back to café cycle blogging. I was worried the blog might not be able to cope if it went quiet for several weeks so came up with a three-point plan.
1.   Get out of the hospital and home
2.   Get better and back cycling as soon as possible
3.   Come up with a plan b to keep the blog going

With a three-point plan in place I could relax and start putting the first point into action.

The good thing was that I was no longer in any pain. There seemed to be two reasons for this, first I had been given a lot of morphine and secondly, I had an epidural in my back providing constant pain relief. No pain was obviously good but there is a side effect from morphine in that it can make you hallucinate a bit. When I closed my eyes to try and sleep all I could see were weird colourful spider images a bit like a Pink Floyd video from the Wall (younger readers should refer to YouTube).

The first time off the bed was to head for a commode but as I had no stomach muscles, seeing as they had been sliced in half, I had to use my arms to push up from a lying position and then try to twizzle round before lowering myself down on to the chair. It was not an easy manoeuvre but highlighted a new problem: for reasons yet unknown, my right arm was completely numb and unusable, and having a dead right arm made pushing myself out of bed almost impossible but I eventually made it. The dead arm was going to prove a bit of a nuisance.

Having now had a drink and been to the loo it meant that I was no longer considered critical so they needed to move me out of Intensive care unit (ITU). In the new area, I would have to share a nurse with another patient. I was happy to be moving out because it meant I was getting better but a little unhappy as I would be going from first class to business class and no one likes being downgraded.

A doctor came to check my arm and concluded that there didn't seem to be permanent nerve damage but recommended a brain scan just in case. Although I was only awake in ITU 36 hours it felt as though I had been there for a very long time.

*****

You don't become an internet sensation by lying in a hospital bed with a tube up your nose, so it was time to start planning my escape.

Outside my room, I heard two doctors talking about their new bikes and rides they had been on. I was pleased when I heard they were only managing 20 miles at a time but I wasn't really in any state to suggest they join me on a longer one.

When the doctors eventually came into my room to check what progress I was making, they agreed I was out of danger. The best news was that I could have my tubes, wires and epidural removed - a good first step for someone wanting to get back to cycling and eating cake.

With tubes removed it was now time to test out how my fitness was after a week in bed, no food and stomach muscles cut in half. It had been less than two weeks since I ran the Barcelona Marathon so how hard could it be to go for a quick jog round the hospital. With the help of a nurse, and a Zimmer frame, I managed to pull myself out of bed and on to my feet. It felt good to be standing up.

For my first post op run I managed an impressive 10 steps (with Zimmer), before I was too knackered to go any further and needed a sit down. A little disappointing and this 'getting fit again after a NDE' was clearly a bit trickier than I thought. I decided that a lie down was in order so retraced my 10 steps back to bed.

*****

The next afternoon, the physiotherapist turned up and gave me lots of obvious information on what I needed to do to recover, which mainly consisted of more walking and resting. She also said it would take at least six months to a year for me to recover. I decided to ignore her recovery timeline, as it didn't fit with my plans.

That evening a bed came free on the proper ward so I was wheeled across. This marked the end of my upgrades and I was now back in cattle class on a budget airline where you had to fend for yourself.

Just as we were leaving Mr Lewis, the surgeon who had cut me in half and whipped out some of my guts, popped in to see how it was going. He thought I had made great progress and as I was eating, walking and pooing he said he thought I could go home the next day, which made me very happy.

After a restless night, I woke up excited that this was the day I expected to get out of hospital. I felt rather proud of my recovery abilities as it had only been a week since I was lying on the floor of the drop-in doctor doing my rolling around in agony party piece. Don't get me wrong I was very impressed with all the doctors and nurses and the fantastic job they had done. After all, without them my NDE would not have included the N part. But at the end of the day a hospital is full of ill people and I didn't want to catch anything. It actually took another two days of hospital procedure before they finally let me go home.

I still had to get another 47,500 visits to the blog and although the count had been slowly ticking over during my forced absence, at the current rate success would still be many years away by which time people may no longer be cycling or eating cake but would be using jet packs and taking food pills instead. I needed to crack on.

Chapter 11
(Visits 2500 only 47,500 to go)

I reviewed my three-point plan.
1. Get out of the hospital and home
2. Get better and back cycling as soon as possible
3. Come up with a plan B to keep the blog going

Step one was complete but step two was evidently going to take a while. Just walking around the outside of the house every hour would leave me breathless and needing a good rest. After a couple of days it started to become a bit easier and I started upping the mileage. The first long walk was almost 200 paces to the end of my road and back, after which I needed a two-hour kip and didn't manage any more walks for the rest of the day. I had another go the next day, adding in an extra lamp post, and I continued with this for the rest of the week. After another week recovery time was down to a couple of hours plus a long afternoon kip.

With this part of my plan now under way I moved on to the blog. I had managed to make it to my pc on my first day back from hospital. It was the only time I can remember writing a post to be physically exhausting, and I needed a rest half way through, but I was determined to explain to my blog fans why there had been no cycling posts recently.

This was what I posted:
I had great plans for cafe cycle reviewing now that spring is here. I had a long list of suggestions of cafes to try, some requests from cafes wishing for me to visit them, there were going to be the first ever European Cafe cycle reviews and the first steps on the 'calorie neutral bike ride' world record attempt.

But why have I put this in the past tense. Well sadly last week I ended up in intensive care with a twisted bowel and have a lovely scar right up my tum to prove it. Fortunately, due to all my cafe cycle riding I am fairly fit and with the healing power of cake, I was able to wake up again a couple of days later and start on the road to recovery.

Although now out of hospital I won't be able to get on a bike for several weeks and then several more weeks to build up long enough rides to include cafe stops.

However, all is not lost as I have a plan B and in this case B is for Bus so for the time being the blog will become a bus cafe review blog.

I'm not up to a bus ride yet but hopefully it won't be too long before Bus Cafe reviewing can start and could even become a regular feature for anyone who doesn't like a nice bike ride before their hot chocolate and cake (although I can't believe that it can ever be the case).

Plan B looked a good one and would allow me to visit some of the local cafes, which I wouldn't have otherwise gone to on a bike ride. As a bonus I thought there might be some people interested in bus café reviewing which could help me on my blog numbers, although as it transpired there aren't and it didn't.

During the next couple of weeks, I started to make slow progress. First, I had the stitches out then I saw my GP for an initial assessment. I asked him how quickly I could start running, cycling and swimming again without splitting in half.

What the doctor said was "it will be at least 6 weeks for cycling and swimming and then to move slowly on to running as it is the hardest, but listen to your body and don't push it or you will end back in hospital."

What I heard was "you will be running again by 6 weeks unless you are a wimp", which was excellent news. He suggested I came back in a month's time before I started any proper exercise so he could give me the all clear.

Encouraged by the doctor's prognosis I started to increase the distance of each long walk but it seemed like slow progress and after 3 weeks I could still only manage a slow half mile followed by a long lie down. I was at least starting to feel less queasy and able to focus while reading or trawling the internet without feeling sick.

As I started to get my strength back I felt it was time to see how close I was to a potential bus-based cafe review. I developed a step by step bus café review process so I could test my current progress against it.
1. Get to bus stop
2. Ride on bumpy bus without splitting in two
3. Get from bus stop to café or tearoom without falling over
4. Sit in café or tearoom long enough to review it without needing a kip
5. Repeat steps 3-1 to get home.

After my daily walking I was confident that I could comfortably achieve step 1. Step 2 seemed difficult to practice as if I got it wrong I would be in serious trouble so I thought I would first have a crack at steps 3 and 4 by walking to the local Waitrose and practicing staying awake in their café.

After a couple of trips I still didn't feel ready for a full bus-based cafe review trip but to keep up momentum I decided to do another trial run to our local Notcutts garden centre cafe. This time I would also be testing point 2 of my process as well. To better replicate a bus-based trip, Chris would play the part of bus driver and drive me there in our bus simulator (or car). To add further to the realism, I waited by the bus simulator for a few minutes before getting on board (it is a single decker bus simulator so I had to sit downstairs).

Once I had alighted from the bus simulator in Notcutts car park we made our way to the cafe. Through habit I ordered a cheese scone, which I regretted as it was very average.

The return ride home was very smooth probably because the bus simulator driver had purchased several house plants and pots and therefore was driving more carefully. At the end of this trip I still needed a short lie down but this time quickly recovered. I even had enough energy to spend another action-packed afternoon sitting in my chair in the garden pointing at weeds that the 'gardener' (who looked very like the bus simulator driver) needed to pull up.

With my bus-based café process trial run check list now complete I felt well enough to try a short bus ride and café stop and could now put plan B into action.

Chapter 12
(Visits 2780 only 47,220 to go)

I had managed to do a couple of posts in the month since I had left hospital and was happy that I was keeping my small band of regular visitors up to date. The blog had now been going 6 months and it had had nearly 3,000 visits but it was not yet the stuff of an internet sensation. Visits had picked up to about 500 a month since the start of the year but thanks to my incapacitation had plateaued at that number.

This was why on a sunny April morning I woke up with an air of anticipation: today was the day to get back on the café comeback trail and more importantly have something to blog about. I knew of a café on the direct bus route from the stop at the end of my road and for my first bus-based cafe review it was perfectly placed. So, accompanied by Chris, I set off for the bus stop.

It wasn't long before a bus turned up and I gingerly climbed on board ready to pay the driver for our trip. As someone who has always used his bike as the primary form of transport (which is free) I was shocked by the cost of a short bus ride (which is not). The quicker I can get back on my bike the cheaper.

We were soon at our stop and alighted (bus speak for got off) heading straight for The Littlehaven Coffee Co., which was tucked away down a side street. It was very nicely laid out inside with a warm and friendly feel.

The first thing I noticed was the choice of hot chocolates, all made from real chocolate rather than powder, and each listed with their % cocoa strength. To demonstrate my macho hot chocolate credentials, I went for an 82% Madagascar, the strongest one. Mr Littlehaven, who was extremely friendly and welcoming, advised that I could also have some flavoured sugar on it (of which there was quite a selection) but I felt that was like having water in your whisky and I wanted it straight.

The hot chocolate was excellent although I think I should have had the sugar sprinkle as 82% is very strong (I didn't let on) and the overall selection of drinks and cakes was extremely good.

On the return bus trip, there was one thing bothering me. I was puzzled why the Littlehaven Coffee Co was in Norwich and not Littlehaven in Wales. I wondered if the coffee beans they used were from the Pembrokeshire coffee plantations but apparently they weren't, which was a shame as the quality of drinks and cake at the Littlehaven Coffee Co. were extremely high so if the café's location was moved to overlook the Pembrokeshire coffee plantations it would be almost perfect.

To be a proper internet sensation you need to keep adding new and interesting features to your on-line output and today's visit had given me another brilliant idea. When Mr Littlehaven thrust The Littlehaven Coffee Co. loyalty card in my hand I thought it would be useful for people to know which cafes had a loyalty scheme and the number of drinks required to qualify for a free one. Rather than just add the details to each post I thought it would be better to have a photo of each loyalty card so I created a little slide show on the blog. I called it my loyalty card picture library feature. How could a constant slide show showing photos of different café loyalty cards not be a sure-fire way to attract people to my blog? Apparently very easily.

*****

My first bus café review had gone so well that a few days later I was ready for a more adventurous trip to the Britannia Cafe run by prisoners from Norwich Prison, where I had agreed to meet Barry and Helen and their tandem. I wanted to let Barry know I was progressing towards my target and that a little thing like a NDE would not stop me from winning the bet. (Although we had to abandon the bus, it being Good Friday, and travel by bus simulator instead).

The ride in the bus simulator went smoothly with the bonus that we didn't need to pick up any passenger simulations at any simulated bus stop or change bus simulator at the half way point, all of which would have been required on a proper bus. It was also a lot cheaper but despite all these advantages it was not the type of bus-based cafe reviewing that I had promised so I arrived at the Britannia Cafe with a heavy heart.

As I alighted the bus simulator Barry and Helen and their tandem pulled up. For dramatic effect, I took extra-long to struggle out of the vehicle and then limped my way to the café entrance. I don't really know why I limped, as my legs hadn't been damaged but I felt it was the best way to signal to everyone that I had been a bit poorly.

The café was extremely busy but, to my horror, devoid of cake. The barista explained that so far that day, the focus had been on breakfast and there had been no time to make any cakes yet despite it being nearly midday.

I told Barry that my blog was now attracting a solid 500 views a month so based on his challenge it would be less than 8 years until I hit his target figure, which was a big improvement since the last time we met. Although I was disappointed with the numbers and the fact I appeared to have plateaued I made it sound like he should be impressed. Of course, he wasn't and with no sign of cake he tried to order a sausage sandwich.

Barry's request was denied as it transpired that we were currently in a café food void, too late for breakfast and too early for cake so all that was available was a scone. The barista also explained that they had had so much recent publicity and good reviews that they were far busier than they had expected to be and were rushed off their feet. I was very pleased for them but it didn't really help our current situation. I was left with no option but to have the scone so at least I would have something to review.

When I returned home I wrote the most positive review I could, seeing as there had been no cake. As my experience had been at odds with everyone else's reviews it was in danger of threatening my café reviewing credibility. Worse still this post quickly became my best read, which probably put a lot of people off my blog. Plan b wasn't going quite as well as I had planned.

*****

Five weeks after I left hospital and despite being told not to do any exercise but walking for at least 6 weeks I couldn't wait any longer. I currently have my oldest road bike attached to an indoor turbo trainer and it had been calling to me for several days. I decided it was time to hop on board and have a little pedal.

Over the next few days progress on the turbo trainer was good and I felt that maybe I would be able to do a proper bike ride soon. In the meantime I decided to try a cafe walking review. I could now do about a 4-mile walk so I got out my map and plotted a circle of 2-mile radius centred on my house to define the target cafe walking zone (TCWZ). Within the TCWZ there was only one candidate: the Modern Life Cafe at the Sainsbury Centre of Visual Arts at the University of East Anglia (UEA) so I decided to walk there.

For those of you who are not culture vultures, you may be surprised to know that the Sainsbury Centre of Visual Arts is not a supermarket but a public art museum originally built to house Lord and Lady Sainsbury's art collection as it had got too big for their front room. For film buffs it was also used as the Avengers' new HQ in their 2015 film.

On arrival, we made our way through the art collection straight to the Modern Life Cafe situated at the far end just past the tinned vegetables and soups.

I was hoping that coming to an art gallery at a university might attract students and art lovers to my blog. As a rule, if a café is good, and I can be positive about it, I seem to get a lot more views than if it is a poor one. Sadly, this was only average so I didn't pull in the new readers I had hoped for.

After I was fully rested we carefully walked home along the river. I informed Chris that if there were no after effects from this trip then I might be able to do a short bike ride for the next cafe visit and cafe cycle reviewing would be back on!

Chapter 13
(Visits to date 3267 only 46,733 to go)

Spring was in the air as the calendar turned to May and I hadn't done a café cycle review for almost 2 months. My plan B (for Bus) reviews had proved successful with blog numbers in April being my best month to date. It was clear that a NDE was what the blog reading public liked to spice up their reads. I didn't feel I would be able to pull off my Lazarus act too often so if I was to become an internet sensation it was clear I needed to return to my core discipline and get back on the bike.

Fortunately, my fitness was improving fast. I still needed lots of afternoon kips but felt things were getting back to normal so it was time for a proper café cycle review.

Being over 6 weeks since my op, I went to ask our GP to give me the exercise thumbs up to start back on the triathlon trail of swimming, running and most importantly cycling outdoors.

I decided the best approach was just to check with him if doing any of these things would do me any harm as I knew I would get an 'it depends' and 'listen to your body' sort of answer which I could easily interpret as 'no, the more the better'. He did say I should do swimming first then move on to the bike before getting back to running.

When I reported in to Chris she said that she would come on a bike ride as soon as I had managed to go swimming so without further ado it was down to the local pool to bang out a few lengths. I returned home in one piece and with the final hurdle ticked off it was at last time to get back on the bike with a little 17-mile loop taking in the River Green Cafe in Trowse just outside of Norwich.

Once back home I had to have a bit of a lie down and afternoon snooze to recover from my exertion, but then it was straight to the

PC to write a rather dull post. It attracted a disappointing number of hits and reinforced that the public wanted something a bit more dramatic.

*****

During the rest of the month I continued to go on some rides increasing in distance each time until it was time to go back to basics and return to the approach I had been using before my NDE: team up with a variety of different guests to visit new places. Poor Chris had had to accompany me on all the bike rides during my recovery to make sure I didn't do anything silly (as if). To give her a break for my next ride I called upon Big George, for a forty-mile trip to a tea room at an actual Hall.

As always Big George had added a layer of logistical challenge to the ride. On this occasion, he had double booked the day by also agreeing to go for a bike ride with his mate Andrew as well. Big George, being a master of the double booking, resolved the situation by inviting Andrew to join us for some cafe cycle reviewing. Therefore, on a bright but windy morning I set off for Earsham Hall Tearooms with cycling guests Big George (double booker) and Andrew (double bookee).

I was keen to show off my navigational skills to a new guest so was very annoyed when my Garmin cycling GPS inexplicably switched itself off. I immediately stopped to restart the device and rectify its malfunction. This was foolish, I had committed the basic tour leader mistake, as you can't lead from the rear (unless you are a general in World War One and that didn't turn out well either). By the time I had satellite navigation again Big George and Andrew had disappeared up the road and gone past the requisite turning required to keep us on route. Once I caught them up and with my navigation credibility already in question I foolishly agreed to press on as my cycling guests insisted that we keep going forward.

With my second mistake of the day now in place we set off again only to find that there appeared to be no suitable turnings off our current road in the direction we required. Eventually we came to a little tarmac track with an 'unsuitable for motorised vehicles' sign. I checked my GPS and although the unsuitable road was not marked on the map it was going in the right direction. As we were not motorised we decided to take it.

This was mistake number three as the road soon ran out and turned into a muddy path. We were still able to cycle on it so we continued until the muddy path became a farmer's field. The correct thing to have done would have been to turn around but by now we couldn't face the indignity of retracing our steps. Instead we got off our bikes and started to push them through the long grass.

After 20 minutes of walking we came to a farmyard where we were stopped by the farmer's boy with a threatening pitch fork who told us to go no further as there were pigs. It appeared that we were meant to understand why this was a problem but as townies we didn't. After all, how much damage can these pigs do to us, we thought.

Just then the farmer's wife, who was out walking her dogs, appeared and politely explained that you can't go through areas of pigs without permission as you could spread pig-based diseases. This made sense and we felt very guilty about bringing our town ways out into the country.

We apologised and promised that we were not planning to go to any more pig farms on our ride today so should be ok. The detour had added 4 miles and 1 hour to the ride. My navigational and leadership credibility was now in tatters, which made it difficult to restore discipline when we needed to get down to some serious hot drink and cake reviewing at the tearoom in the hall.

As we tucked into our refreshments Andrew became very confused as I asked him for his marks out of 10. He wasn't expecting a rating-based interrogation so it was no surprise that Andrew (Double bookee) never came on one of my rides again.

*****

With confidence growing it was now time to re-introduce the sportive rides as this was not only a great way to get a group of people on a ride but more importantly also viewing the blog.

On this occasion, I had contacted anyone I knew who had a bike and was pleased, if a little surprised to see Chris's friend Rachael had signed up to come along. Rachael had never been a great cycling fan so on studying the details of the route she had suggested a point where she could join the ride and then accompany the rest of the group to the café.

On the morning of the ride, six of us lined up at race HQ and we duly met up with Rachael after about six miles of our thirty-six-mile loop.

The ride went smoothly for the next few miles but then Rachel's lack of practice caught up with her as she started to flag and kept saying that she assumed it wasn't much further to the cafe. It became apparent that due to a miscommunication she had thought we were going the other way around the loop and was expecting a 5-mile rather than a 25-mile ride. Chris kindly stepped in to attempt to resolve the situation by first offering Rachel her drink and then, when that ran out, by starting to lie about how much further it was to the cafe. This worked well for a bit until the lies wore off and the miles clocked up with no coffee in sight.

Luckily, we had several riders with us who were experienced in riding in groups and knew how to lead out a tiring rider. Without further instruction, we impressively got into formation and each took our turn at lying to Rachel, with a continually more convincing 'we really are nearly there now' honest', until we safely arrived at the cafe. It is no surprise that Rachael never came on one of my rides again.

With the partial success of my group ride strategy I quickly arranged another, which this time included Jodie as one of the party. Using my useful routes facility on the blog, regular sportive guest Ali had managed to download the day's route on to his newly purchased GPS. His face lit up when I said he could be assistant deputy navigator for the day. He was disappointed that the role didn't come with a special assistant deputy navigator hat but took it on all the same. With the focus being on hats I hadn't realised that he didn't yet know how to follow a route on his device, which was a serious oversight.

As the ride got underway I assumed that my assistant deputy navigator was busy at the front of the group performing navigational duties. This gave me the opportunity to perform lead rider duties by making sure I chatted with all today's participants and pretended to be interested in what they had been up to in the last week. Whilst chatting to Jodie I saw the assistant deputy navigator miss the correct turning. Due to the number of times that missing a turn had led to follow up issues I naturally yelled 'wrong way' and slammed on my brakes. Jodie hadn't been expecting this so was startled and crashed into the back of my bike, tipping her straight into a ditch of nettles. As she was being stung she started to squeal that her foot was stuck in the pedal and couldn't get free. Although I acted as quickly as I could I was not able to get my phone out quick enough and she had managed to free herself before I could get a picture of her in the ditch for the blog. It is no surprise that Jodie never came on one of my rides again.

*****

Before the NDE Big George and I had been planning a cycle ride to France to find the best café anywhere between London and Paris (that we happened to stop at). Now I was back up to speed the trip could still go ahead. The route I planned would require us to ride 100 miles on two of the days. I thought it might be a good idea if we did some actual training as it had been a long time since either of us had ridden that far. For a first long ride, I suggested a 66-mile loop down to Wortham in North Suffolk where there just happened to be a tea shop we could pop into for a sneaky cafe cycle review. Just before we were due to meet up I got a text from Big George apologising that he would have to cancel due to a work commitment. I still wanted to do the ride so I asked my Imaginary Friend if he would come instead.

We set off on a fantastic summer's day and raced down to the Norfolk- Suffolk border.

My Imaginary friend doesn't say much so without the normal chit chat we soon arrived at the Wortham Tearooms and went inside where I got some funny looks from the waitress when I asked for a table for two and I got a further look when I ordered a hot chocolate as my drink on a boiling hot day but this is the way of a café cycle reviewer

When it arrived, I noticed that the cake had been served on top of the serviette. This course of action inevitably ends up with the napkin being covered in crumbs and icing thus rendering it useless for its primary purpose of wiping sticky fingers and mouth. I therefore had to take great care eating the cake to avoid the need to wipe away crumbs (which I think I accomplished rather well).

It was a serious issue and I wanted to make sure less accomplished cake eaters didn't face the same challenge. I immediately started a campaign to name and shame any establishments that served cake in this way to try and eliminate this outrageous practice. I called it #keepcakeoffserviettes and my second café campaign was born. Nonetheless, the quality of food and drink, plus the large number of cakes on offer made this a very pleasant stop. Despite this it is no surprise that imaginary friend never came on one of my rides again.

I seemed to be losing potential cycling guests, and therefore potential blog readers, at an alarming rate so decided to return to my reliable guests, such as Andrew (who is notoriously hard to please) for my next few rides.

Now I was back on regular blogging I was pleased to note that the month of May had been by far my best to date with six new posts and over a thousand visits for the first time. It was important to keep up the output in June because if I had an equally successful month I would hit the magic five thousand mark and be a tenth of the way there, even if it had taken over a quarter of my allotted time.

Chapter 14
(Visits 4089 only 45,911 to go)

With the small increase in visitors I began to feel under pressure to make sure each trip had a worthwhile incident or useful fact to post about as I felt that pictures of coffee and cake might not be enough to keep people engaged.

I wasn't disappointed with the worthwhile incident contribution from my next ride with Andrew (who is notoriously hard to please). It all started as a normal ride from HTPH. We were going to go to Wiveton Hall on the North Norfolk coast. The way up was uneventful, as Andrew ranted on about the quality of vegetarian sausage rolls, however things soon changed once we arrived.

We rode down the long shingle drive to the café where I locked our bikes up with Alarmio. Wiveton Hall Café can be busy so I was keen we got a table and headed straight inside. It was first straight to the counter to check out the cakes and award the effective cake selection (ECS) score. Whilst considering the excellent choice available a lady rushed in frantically asking whose bike was beeping. I went to investigate foolishly leaving Andrew alone at the counter. It appeared that Alarmio had been disturbed by a strong wind, which it had mistaken for a bicycle thief and gone off. I reset it before sheepishly sneaking back inside.

On returning to the ECS rating activity I was concerned to find that Andrew had already ordered a cappuccino plus a beetroot hummus and carrot sandwich but no cake. As a beetroot hummus and carrot sandwich isn't a cake he had unintentionally excluded himself from the cake rating part of our visit. Stepping up to the plate I was now forced to order two cakes to score myself. With a fabulous selection I made my choices only to discover that all was not well on the beetroot hummus and carrot sandwich front.

Despite it clearly stating that lunch was available from 12:00, Andrew had broken all the rules and attempted to order his sandwich at 11:53. Quite rightly he was refused as clearly an early sandwich would cause chaos in the Wiveton Hall Cafe kitchen. Andrew protested and after some lengthy negotiations, lasting just over seven minutes, it was agreed he could have his beetroot hummus and carrot sandwich after all. He sat there smugly gloating over his victory while I got down to the matter in hand by rating the café and updating my 'café's rating spreadsheet on my phone.

*****

By mid-summer and I felt I was getting back into the swing of cycle café reviewing again although it was beginning to get a bit samey especially as every ride couldn't guarantee the excitement of a beetroot hummus and carrot sandwich incident. It was time to spice things up a bit and look further afield for potential blog readers. I arranged a brain storming session and after some serious flip chart work I had the brilliant idea to take my café cycle reviewing ways to le continent.

I left no time in arranging the first expedition as I packed a tent, family and guest reviewers Barry and Helen and their tandem into the car and headed straight for the Netherlands where cycling and cafés are a way of life.

This would not be a one-off trip into Europe but the first of four over the summer months at the end of which I would be able to crown the European cafe of the year as well as having improved my overall cycle cafe rating skills with international experience.

After the best night's sleep that is possible when you are my age and sleeping on a mat on the hard ground in a cold tent, I rounded the troops up ready for my first café cycling experience outside the UK. I felt it important to make sure everyone was prepared for the differences that they would encounter when cycling here so I gave a full briefing including which side of road to cycle on and the need to speak louder when talking to anyone. Barry and Helen and their tandem had been to this part of Holland before and so I put them in charge of routes. For the first trip, they had planned a 30-mile, two stop introductory route so with Chris and sons Peter and George in tow we set off.

There are many more cycle paths and cyclists in this part of the world but for some reason the Dutch seem to like to cobble their smaller roads to make cycling a little harder than it need be. This, combined with the wind against, made the first part of the ride rather slow but we eventually arrived at the first stop, Central cafe in Baaralo.

When back in Britain you get a wide range of possible potential stops on your cycle ride. At one end of the refreshment option continuum is the spit and sawdust pub whilst at the other is the olde worlde tea shop. In the Netherlands, nearly every establishment fits right in the middle of the refreshment option continuum and would be described as a cafe bar. This meant that home-made cake was not on offer and the preferred drink was Trappist beer rather than hot chocolate or coffee. The international guide to cafe cycle reviewing suggested the following simplified scoring system for use on the continent: Just rate drink, food and ambiance. Drink had to either be Trappist beer or a hot drink. People selecting standard drinks like fizzy water, coke, juice or larger would take no part in the drink rating part of cycle cafe reviewing as these things always tasted the same. They seemed like good rules so I immediately informed my cycling guests, who appeared unbothered about this revelation.

The Central cafe in Baaralo, had some excellent food and drink but we struggled to concur on our atmosphere and ambiance thinking. Despite my protests that the ambiance lacked something, as the Central cafe over looked the central car park, the others all liked the feel of the place, clearly swept up with the romance of cycling abroad. Barry thought the ambiance was good as the car park became a market on a Thursday but as today was a Tuesday I didn't really know why this was relevant from an ambiance perspective.

We eventually reached a compromise and the central cafe in Baaralo had scored surprisingly well with a 7.67. It was currently the best café anywhere in Europe and had set the bar for the rest to live up to.

With the first ever foreign cycle café review in the pannier it was time to set off to our next destination. On the way we passed through several villages each with lots of cafés but they all looked a bit alike. You soon get to realise that the village set up across Holland is rather formulaic. Village square by big church with bandstand type thing in the middle and cafés round the outside

Barry had chosen the village of Panningen for our second stop and using the standard Dutch layout we easily found the requisite row of cafés. We selected Café Dakepello as it had most people sitting in the compulsory continental style outdoor seating pavement area. It was a bit cold and drizzly but I insisted we sat outside so that we could blend in. It was also my first opportunity to try a Dutch hot chocolate as I had spotted it on the menu. To go with it I selected strawberry flan.

I must report that the whole experience turned out to be rather disappointing as my drink was an anaemic milky offering and the strawberry flan flattered to deceive. I discovered that the Dutch equivalent to a Cadbury's drinking chocolate was something called Chocomel and best avoided. The ambiance wasn't great here either as the only view was of other cafés and modern shops as well as being very noisy. If the central cafe Baaralo had set the bar, then Café Dakepello had little difficulty limbo dancing right under it.

As we set off again it started to rain but despite the soaking I felt this was a good start to my European adventure. As soon as we got back I whipped out my IPad ready to update the blog using the campsite wifi network. I was hoping the novelty of the trip would attract new readers but I hadn't really thought it through.

It was clear that back in Blighty my blog readers often came from people searching for information on a café they wanted to go to. When they entered the café name on a Google search my post would pop up luring them to my blog. I had also mastered the trick of posting on the visited 'café's Facebook pages to generate further interest. None of these things were available to me here so it turned out only my most loyal followers could be bothered to read this post and it attracted a very low count.

Exhausted from lack of sleep, cycling and posting I headed for the floor hoping that it would be a more comfortable night.

For the next day's ride Barry and Helen and their tandem had planned another double cafe 40-mile session. It was a lovely Dutch morning as we set off on our bikes. The main excitement on the way to the first stop was a river crossing where I reluctantly paid the ferryman before we got to the other side.

I had high hopes as we arrived at De Ijsvogel (kingfisher mill) just outside Arcen. It looked a much nicer stop than yesterday's offerings with a big courtyard on the side of a water mill. But the drinks and food let down the setting, especially as it was Chocomel again on the hot chocolate front.

The De Ijsvogel scored ok but should have done better for such a good location and couldn't knock the overrated central cafe, Baaralo from the top spot.

To make cycling easier the Dutch have come up with an ingenious yet simple cycle route planning solution. It involves networks of numbered points, each point spread out every few kilometres on the quite roads and cycle paths. Then using a special cycle map with all the number points on it, you just plan which numbers you will visit on your route and follow them. To make it even easier there are direction signs along the roads showing the way to each numbered point.

It is therefore almost impossible to go wrong so it was surprising just how many times Barry and Helen and their tandem got lost. On one occasion this was apparently because the Dutch had suddenly built a motorway across the cycle path blocking our way

It was very busy in Horst town square, which had a big screen set up for Holland's World Cup games but better still was currently showing the Tour de France.

We chose our seat in the compulsory outdoor pavement seating area of Passi cafe and waited some time to place our order. For once there was a different hot chocolate available. This time the chocolate came on a stick and you melted it yourself into the hot milk provided. They also had strawberry waffles so I was optimistic of a good cycle cafe rating.

I was happy but Barry and Helen and their tandem reckoned that the beer was only average and although the hot chocolate was much better than the Chocomel of previous stops, it was not very hot or chocolatey. The strawberry waffles were very nice but a bit small and, I was reliably informed, not as good as the ones at overrated central cafe Baaralo.

I thought the ambiance was excellent as I could clearly see the Tour de France on the big screen but the rest of the group thought the overrated central cafe Baaralo was better despite the fact it over looked a car park. I reluctantly agreed that if you took away the big screen then the setting here was a bit car parky too so couldn't knock the Central café from the top of the league.

*****

I woke to the sound of rain lashing down outside the tent. I know that one of the golden rules of camping is to make sure you never get cold and wet as once you are you are unlikely to ever warm up properly. When this has happened to me I have tried every way to get warm again - a hot shower, staying in my sleeping bag all day or warming each part of my body in turn under the hot air drier in the campsite toilet block but have found none of these effective. Warmth only returns when back in your own house with controllable central heating.

I spent day three cold and wet looking out of the tent window playing various card games. On the positive side, I did receive an e-mail from my mother. I assumed she had read the latest post and was concerned about my toothache which I had mentioned in it, but it was just to tell me dessert is spelt with two s's and not one. I told her that the pain killers had started to work so the pain was now manageable although sadly there is nothing I could take to improve my spelling or grammar.

Next morning, the rain continued to come down and finding the European cafe of the year was getting nowhere. It was time to give myself a serious talking to and I decided to man up. I told my fellow bored cycling guests that however hard it was raining I would set out to find a cafe at 12:30 (Central European time).

When the allotted time arrived, I undertook a short pitch inspection before declaring conditions were now fit for a ride as it was only raining a bit. Much to my surprise the rest of the party agreed to come along as well as they too were out of their minds with boredom.

My timing had been perfect as I had stumbled across the only lull in the rain all day. The rain lull didn't last long and soon after we set off it got heavier giving us all a good drenching on the way to our potential stop.

Pedalling hard we tried to avoid getting too wet which at least meant it was not long before we got to the Morgenstond cafe by a river.

Like all Dutch cafe bars, it was rather dark inside but there was still a good ambiance and nice view of the storm from the window.

To warm up I immediately opted for a hot chocolate only to find that it was the weak and wishy washy Chocomel. I couldn't face another one of those so instead I decided to risk a Trappist beer and pain killer cocktail.

The food here was good so despite the rain the Morgenstond cafe had turned out to be an excellent stop and was the new official best cafe in the whole of Europe.

Outside the monsoon was now only torrential rain so we set off back to the camp site. After two days of solid rain it was sometimes hard to tell the difference between the road and the river running next to it but with a bit of help from the wind we made good time back to the campsite to complete a nineteen-mile round trip.

The next morning, my toothache had completely gone and the weather looked set fair for the day but as it was going to be the last ride in Holland I was leaving no stone left unturned in making sure we had two top café contenders to check out. Therefore Barry and I, armed with a map and a pin, held an in-depth pre-ride planning session to select our destination and route.

Last night had been the world cup semi-final between our hosts and Argentina. It had not ended well. This is the cruel world of the penalty shootout.

On the way to the first planned stop we passed a famous windmill. We knew it was famous as it said so on my map. No one knew why it was famous as it looked like all the others. Maybe it was the one that had a little mouse with clogs on in it (but it wasn't).

Our first stop was in Bassel where we had a choice of cafés. I referenced my Dutch village check-list: big church tick, near central square tick, with bandstand tick, must be some cafe bars nearby tick. We chose Hererg de Bonged as it had the best beer sign.

Sadly only Chocomel was available as the hot chocolate so I was forced down the local Trappist beer road. I was pleased I did as it was very good and had gone almost as soon as it arrived. We all agreed this was excellent beer and scored it appropriately high.

As always Holland's national dish of bacon and cheese pancakes were on offer but little consensus of how they compared with the ones at yesterday's stop. The argument went on for some time before I sensibly gave them the same score and called it a pancake draw.

The Hererg de Bonged in Bassel had done well in each category but with only a standard Dutch village square view it did not become best cafe in Europe.

After another ferry crossing we came to our second stop at the D'hefren van Bafrlo cafe on the outskirts of Baaralo. It had the nicest view of any European cafe to date as it overlooked the river crossing and town. With an excellent ambiance rating then if it could do well in food and drink it could become the new leader.

Things didn't start well with only Chocomel, and bottled beer leading to a poor drinks score. Still a 10 out of 10 on the desserts would get D'hefren van Bafrlo cafe to the number one spot.

As we waited for the fruit pies and ice creams to turn up you could feel the same tension growing as there had been in the campsite bar waiting for the outcome of the World Cup penalty shootout. Most of the desserts hit the back of the net. Cherry pie - Goal, chocolate sundae - Goal, apricot meringue type thing - Goal, Blueberry cheesecake - Goal. It just needed Helen's fruit sundae surprise to score and put D'hefren van Bafrlo to the top of the league. When it arrived the surprise part of the pudding turned out to be that the fruit was out of a tin rather than the fresh selection of local berries she had expected and it was blasted over the bar for a big miss!

Once again it had not turned out well for the locals as D'hefren van Bafrlo was robbed of the prize at the death so I was pleased to see that the orange bunting around the cafe was being taken down as we left.

In terms of blog visits then my first European adventure had been a big flop. Barry had continued to be rude about the blog throughout the trip and claimed that the low hit rate while in Holland had just proved his point. Deep down I started to think he might be right but felt I still owed it to Europe to carry on searching.

Chapter 15
(Visits 5547 only 44,453 to go)

I wasn't going to be back in the UK for long before it would be time to set off on the next leg in the search for the best café in Europe but before I left I had some other café cycle business to take care of. Most urgent was to catch up with Big George so we could discuss progress and plans for our ride from London to Paris in a few weeks' time. This would obviously be done as part of a fifty-mile café cycle ride.

Big George surprisingly turned up on time for the start of our meeting and seemed in good form as we headed south but his mood soon changed as he seemed to be struggling to keep up. To help motivate him I told him about the training I had done and planned to do before our trip. In return he told me why he hadn't had time to do any training yet. He assured me that this was not going to be a problem as even though he was about to go away to Portugal for a two-week family holiday there was still plenty of time to fit in lots of training in the week before we go.

I wasn't convinced by his plan but to keep up morale I assured him that he would be fine as we continued to cruise along (slowly) until we reached The Three Willows café near Bungay.

I quickly did the cake reviewing, ordered our drinks and cake before taking a seat outside in the sunshine so we could continue to plan our Paris trip. Big George again surprised me by claiming that he had been doing a lot of in depth internet research. To save time I asked him for his top three findings. They were:
1. Paris is in France
2. You must go over or under a lot of sea to get to France
3. The people in France mainly speak a language called French, which Big George claimed he could speak. Tres Bon.

As a last-ditch attempt to encourage Big George to shape up I tried doing some cycle training cramming on the way home by going extra fast. This didn't have the desired effect as he soon started to fade and we had to slow down again. I feared that we might not make it to Paris although after our next ride it really became clear what size of challenge I was up against.

*****

It was now getting towards the end of July and the blog had passed the 5,000 views landmark, encouraging me to see if I could make a real breakthrough. I was to fly to Slovenia to continue the search for the best café in the whole of Europe (as long as it was fairly near to where I was staying).

On this trip, I would be joined by my family plus my brother Duncan and his family, which reminded me that I needed to get back to planning my calorie neutral bike ride world record attempt. With all my recent focus on my recovery, getting posting again and the search for European café of the year I had put this challenge to the back of my mind.

We arrived at our apartment in Kranjska Gora a few days before Duncan's group turned up so it was important not to waste potential riding opportunities. On our first day, I planned a route to see if Slovenia could give us a contender for the European café of the year title.

The ride was going to take in a steep climb up towards the Austrian border before heading back down to the small village of Mojstrana. Today's cycling guests were Chris and George (younger son). Once eldest son Peter had discovered that some serious uphill pedalling would be involved he decided he would rather stay in bed and wait for flatter options.

Soon we were breathlessly pedalling our mountain bikes up stone tracks with gears running out fast. The views were stunning and almost worth the pain. In fact, I was enjoying it so much I missed the signpost for the route we were meant to be taking which resulted in us going the wrong way up a very steep bit.

After about 20 minutes I realised that something didn't seem right, as we seemed to be heading away from the village where our café-stop was. I decided to consult my map where it immediately became obvious that I had made a directional error. Unfortunately, cyclable paths half way up mountains are in short supply and our only option was to turn around and go back the way we came.

My how my cycling guests cheerily laughed on hearing the news that the last twenty painful minutes of effort had been for nothing.

As we continued on up my cycling guests started to suffer, complaining of sore knees and backs and that sweat was dripping down places that it ought not to be.

Once at the top we rested, refuelled and admired the views before it was downhill all the way to our café stop at the Gostinstvo in turizem café in Mojstrana. You would have thought that going down would be a lot less painful than climbing up. Surprisingly, this is not the case. If you are to avoid racing out of control and over the edge of the path to a certain death in the valley below you must go down squeezing your brakes very tightly. Inevitably leading to aching and cramping fingers and far more rests than on the way up.

With our legs very tired and fingers very sore, we eventually got to our stop and parked our bikes. Considering the stunning views on offer along the route, the Gostinstvo in turizem cafe was a little disappointing as all the mountains were hidden by the surrounding buildings, although it did get an extra half point for having a proper table tennis table in its outdoor seating area.

After the disappointment of the poor quality hot chocolate available in Holland it was good to find a nice one here. There was also refreshing beer and grapefruit shandy available for my guests so drinks scored reasonably well.

On the food front, there was only ice cream on offer but for the café to qualify for European Café of the Year food must be tested and we weren't putting in all this effort only to find this café had been disqualified. Therefore, for food I ordered a banana split flavoured ice cream and George a strawberry and Milka (alpine chocolate) one. We thought they were ok but Chris claimed the strawberry ice cream was the most disgusting ice cream she had ever had, as it tasted more like medicine. As she hadn't ordered any food her rating of -100 didn't count.

I had enjoyed the ride but the café had been a disappointing start to the alpine leg of the search for the best cafe in all of Europe. Fortunately the good hot chocolate meant Gostinstvo in turizem cafe just avoided the European wooden spoon.

The next day Duncan and co were due to arrive but I decided there wasn't time to hang around and form a welcoming committee when another café review was out there waiting to be done. For this one I decided to go on a mini European tour to give several countries the chance to offer up the winner. Starting in Slovenia we would ride through Italy and then into Austria to find a suitable cycle cafe to review. There was no pre-chosen café destination as so far this approach had not come up with the goods. I would put café selection in the hands of fate to see if this would produce the exceptional European café I was hoping to find. The route would all be on cycle track and therefore flat. Today's guests were Chris, George and Peter (son who will only come if there are no uphill bits).

We set off along the cycle path in Slovenia before arriving at the Italian border, where we rode through some lovely woods on the way to Austria. It was a very pleasant ride and it was great to be able to sample the different cultures that each country offered (although we had only gone 12-miles).

Once into Austria I hoped fate would guide us to a suitable Austrian cycle cafe to review. We hadn't gone far when fate delivered the goods and brought us to Gasthof Wanker. I will be very disappointed if any of you think that I decided to stop there just because the café had a smutty name, it was fate that brought us here.

We parked our bikes outside. With me and the boys still sniggering and Chris telling us to grow up, we went inside. It was typically alpine and very dark but there was a nice patio area with a super view out the back so I awarded a good atmosphere and ambiance score and we were off to a flying start.

Even though it was very hot George stepped up to the plate and agreed to have the requisite hot chocolate while I had a cold beer. The beer was good but the hot chocolate was average being disappointingly weak.

Like a lot of Alpine establishments, the food menu was rather limited and only had various meat with chips. All the other punters were having some type of schnitzel so we all did as well. The stuffed schnitzel was better than the breadcrumb one, which in turn was better than plain but basically it was just bashed up meat. On the positive side, I was pleased to see 1980's favourite the crinkle cut chip was still in fashion here.

Gasthof Wanker was a good stop but nothing special and sadly (or fortunately) we won't be seeing its name on the European cafe of the year winner's certificate. Hopefully fate has learnt that there is more to selecting a good café than just finding one with a smutty name.

There was a choice of routes for the way back. Either the safe option of going back the way we came or the adventurous option of taking the bikes up to the Austria / Slovenia border on a chair lift, allowing one to cycle back down the mountain through the woods. Chris decided on the safe route (so here her story ends), while the rest of the party correctly knew that you never go back on a cycle ride (unless you are lost) and opted for the chair lift approach.

We cycled down to the chairlift and waited behind four old age cyclists (OACs) who were planning to do the same thing.

We watched the OACs carefully to see how you get on a chairlift with a bike. It was a bit of a shock to find that you had to sit on the dangly chair and cling on to your bike which was not strapped on to the chairlift in any way but balanced on the foot rest.

I felt sure that one of us or the OACs would drop their bikes so was relieved to make it to the top with our bikes surprisingly still intact and set off on a straight forward ride down the mountain before meeting up back at our Slovenian apartment.

*****

By now we had been joined by my brother's family so there would be eight guest reviewers ready for the next leg of my alpine adventure. Over dinner I brought Duncan up to speed with progress to date and the planned route for the next day, whilst he fell asleep into his goulash.

Next morning the weather was perfect for a European café search and with bikes hired for my new cycling guests we were ready to go. Like a scene from the sound of music, minus the singing and the nuns, we set off on bikes down a purpose-built cycle path.

The route went along what I consider to be the best stretch of cycle path in the world. It is on an old railway line that ran between Slovenia and Italy with meadows and mountains on either side. It is mainly flat but with a short uphill sting in the tail to take you up to the lakes. This meant that when we arrived at the imaginatively named Lago 1 (Lake 1) everyone was a bit out of breath.

We parked our bikes before a pleasant stroll round the small but very pretty lake before deciding to follow the signs to the rather more descriptively named Lago 2 (Lake 2) for lunch.

Although both lakes (lagos) had cafés neither looked like potential winners of the European cafe of the year title so not wanting to waste the opportunity I suggested we head back to Slovenia and try out the better-looking prospect of Hotel Vitranc which we had passed on the way.

Hotel Vitranc is in the charming village of Podkoren and has an excellent outdoor seating area with comfy chairs.

Unfortunately, you can't see any mountains from the outdoor seating area but you know they are there which gives a calm relaxing feel to the place. To more than make up for the lack of mountain view you can see an apartment once featured in Channel 4's excellent property/travel series: A place in the sun (series 3 episode 12). Sitting here we were following in the footsteps of top property/travel presenter Amanda Lamb who may have once also had a drink and sat in the comfy chairs in the outdoor seating area at the Hotel Vitranc. I wondered what drink and food she would have chosen but sadly there was no plaque marking the occasion, which I felt to be an oversight. It all added up to a high mark for ambiance and atmosphere.

We ordered drinks, which were mainly beer and coke although for reviewing purposes I also ordered a hot chocolate. All of them were very good meaning that a good display on the food front could see the Hotel Vitranc go to the top of the European leader board.

Apple strudel and ice cream seemed to be the order of the day and were top draw so thanks to an 8.5 food rating suddenly the Hotel Vitranc Slovenia was officially the best cafe in the whole of Europe beating anything Holland, Italy or Austria had to offer.

I was pleased to find a decent café worthy of winning the European cafe of the year but the award was not yet in the bag as I still had more Alpine venues to check out and there would be further opportunities when I cycled to Paris with Big George in a months' time.

With three rides in the bag my cycling guests all thought that there had been enough of this 'Café cycle nonsense' so it was a few days before I could persuade the group back on to their bikes again.

As it turned out it was well worth it from a blog visitor view point as the ride ended up producing what continues to be one of my most successful posts of all time which was still attracting regular hits over a year later. It is a bit of a mystery as to why as it was a rather dull ride to a poor venue. We had cycled to the nearest Italian town in a light drizzle and then made a bad choice to go to an average pizza house. Worse still it had run out of hot chocolate. I did my best to write an interesting post from the very limited material but gave it the good Italian title of Mama Mia.

Ever since this post has got hits every day. I can only think that making the title the same as an Abba song had drummed up unexpected interest from fans of the Swedish Eurovision winners. I decided to build on this success by naming a number of other posts after other Abba hits but without any noticeable similar increase in blog traffic. Once again I remain none the wiser although grateful for the push towards my internet sensation goal.

It continues to be a disappointment that none of my posts about the European adventures ever attracted much interest, as they were some of my favourite rides. It did reinforce the view of some people, that: "no one wants to read about where you cycle to or what cake you eat. The only reason there are any visits, other than family and friends, is that you have produced a useful list of cafes in Norfolk and Suffolk". I was still determined to show these people that they were wrong.

As our time in the mountains drew to a close it looked like my alpine cycling was done. Then, much to my surprise George (son) and Jake (nephew) announced they would like to ride up the 7.5 mile 24 hairpin bend Vršič mountain pass as a challenge. This sounded a great idea as I suspected there would be a cafe at the top so I invited myself along and made them my guest reviewers for the ride.

It is easy to be tricked by the weather in the mountains but the sun was shining and there were no clouds about so it looked like a good opportunity to make our cycling ascent. In Slovenia, the climb up Vršič is legendary and is similar to how the French talk about Alpe d'heuz. There are often races up it and always cyclists on the road taking on the challenge. As we set off I knew it was going to be tough so to help inspire and motivate my cycling guests I sang the lyrics to Miley Cyrus's classic 'The Climb'.

There's always going to be another mountain
I'm always gonna wanna make it move

Always going to be an uphill battle,
Sometimes I'm gonna have to lose,
Ain't about how fast I get there,
Ain't about what's waiting on the other side
It's the climb

Although I have since been able to look up the correct lyrics, at the time the only line I actually knew was 'it's the climb' so I had to dum-de-dum the other bits and then just belt out 'it's the climb' every few minutes when I got to that part of the song. As you can imagine this was very motivational and thus we made good progress towards the top.

After about an hour of solid up I noticed the sun had disappeared and the sky had darkened meaning a soaking was on the cards. Years of cycling practice, including forcing my children to cycle with me, meant George and I still had a bit in the tank so as soon as it started to rain, unlike the marines, we were prepared to leave a man behind if it meant not getting wet and we left Jake to struggle up the last bit without us, or my inspirational singing.

As the rain got heavier we kindly waited for Jake at the top in the dry of cafe Tučarjev dom.

Inside was very dark and not very welcoming. Due to the wait for Jake we got beaten to the front of the café queue by a coach party of old people, I think Italian, all waving their tokens for coffee and strudel which were clearly included in the price of their excursion.

When we did eventually get our hot chocolate, strudel and a seat each item turned out to be faintly disappointing with only the lemon zest twist in the apple strudel saving cafe Tučarjev Dom from becoming the worst cafe in all of Europe.

We waited for the rain to ease before flying back down the slippery roads in only 25 minutes. It was a shame to have put in so much effort for such a poor cafe visit. But then I remembered the words of Miley:
Ain't about what's waiting on the other side
It's the climb

Suddenly I understood what she meant; it was the fun and enjoyment of cycling uphill with aching legs and burning lungs for 90 minutes that was important and not the rubbish cafe at the top.

The search for European café of the year had gone well but I clearly had not captured the reader's imagination. It was time to return to the UK and come up with a new plan.

Chapter 16
(Visits 6,682 only 43,318 to go)

There was now less than a month to go before my next cycling challenge; the much talked-about trip to find the best café anywhere between London and Paris (that we happen to stop at). I wanted to cram in as many cycling opportunities as possible to make sure I was in peak shape for the trip. So, during August, I managed another seven café cycle rides to post about.

On the longest of these I had the opportunity to kill two proverbial birds with one metaphoric stone. First bird was to appease Andrew who had recently taken a day trip to Cambridge where he had been taken to a 'fantastic' Italian café, which he recommended I reviewed asap. The second bird was the chance to do a much-needed London to Paris long training ride. I therefore decided to repeat the 80-mile Cambridge ride I did last year with Big George and hey presto two birds stoned to death.

As the wind was from the west we chose to get the train to Cambridge and cycle back with the wind helping us along. The train journey was disappointingly uneventful as I listened to Andrew whinge and moan about the lack of investment in rail infrastructure so I was pleased when we arrived and could get down to the business of the day.

It was a short cycle from the station to Savino's Italian cafe in the centre of Cambridge. On his previous visit Andrew had not gone by bike so we managed to get lost amongst the Cambridge University colleges before we eventually found the prospective Italian gem we were looking for. I must say that on arrival it was not what I expected. It looked just like a typical cafe but with an Italian name. Andrew may be hard to please but he is a sucker for anything Italian so had clearly been fooled by the Italian name, painted il Tricolores and the generic continental accents of the staff.

Still Andrew had brought me here for the excellent cake so I went inside to review what was on offer. To my surprise there were no cakes on display, I couldn't even take a photo of the choice available. I hadn't come all this way just for an imitation Italian café so I bravely asked the waitress if there was in fact any cake. She said it was in the Italian kitchen and they had Italian carrot cake, Italian lemon drizzle cake or Italian chocolate and almond cake available. I went for Italian chocolate and almond cake.

Andrew thought his coffee was great, mainly because it was Italian although they could have served him warmed up dish water and he still would have raved about it, but my Italian hot chocolate was far too milky. I did have to admit that the Italian chocolate and almond cake was very good but I'm not sure it was worth the £16.90 train ticket and the 80-mile bike ride home.

*****

With just a week to go before my next adventure I decided it was time to check out how Big George's training had been going to make sure he would be match fit for our trip. A lot was resting on this as it was the last chance for a café to snatch the coveted European Café of the year crown and as it would be an iconic ride I was confident it would attract a big blog following.

Just before my NDE I had been asked if I could advise on a suitable bike route from Norwich Cathedral to Little Walsingham in North Norfolk for some people who were looking to set up a Pilgrims way for bikes. Apparently Little Walsingham is Norfolk's answer to Lourdes in France and lots of people make the pilgrimage every year. I believe your average pilgrim walks or pops along in the car, however if any of them wanted to go by bike this was the route the pilgrimage people had come up with.

I felt very honoured to have been asked to ride it in a consultancy capacity. I promised I would check it out from a cyclist's rather than pilgrim's viewpoint. Sadly, the week I had originally planned to do it was when I ended up in hospital, but this seemed an ideal opportunity to try out the 75-mile loop.

The route needed to go past several churches, which are apparently a must when you are on a pilgrimage, so we wound our way through many Norfolk villages on one of the best cycle routes I had done.

After struggling into a headwind all the way we finally arrived at Little Walsingham, which I found to be more creepy than spiritual. It reminded me of the village in League of Gentlemen but with more nuns. There are lots of shops which sell cheap and tacky religious memorabilia – if you need a plastic Jesus this is the place to come. We headed straight for the Our Lady of Walsingham tourist centre where there were information leaflets, plus cafe where I could do a quick cafe cycle review.

The Cafe was a bit dark inside and the outside seating area only offered a view of a wall and Little Walsingham high street but given the choice we decided to sit outside. With seating sorted and bikes secured it was time to return inside where we found a very good-looking cake selection. I ordered honey cake and Big George excitedly went for banana cake as he claimed to have a lot of banana cake experience.

Due to the slow progress on the way up I was now in a hurry to get back home as I had urgent golf arranged for the evening. With the wind behind, and having done several long rides recently, I felt the 35-mile ride would easily be accomplished in time. In my calculations, I hadn't accounted for Big George falling apart as, despite having eaten all his banana cake, he first had an achy knee and then a series of cramp attacks.

After about 20 miles he said he needed to stop and got off the bike, which ended with him sitting on the side of the road massaging his legs. I knew that if I stayed with him to make sure he got home safely then I would miss my golf. As I contemplated what to do, I was overwhelmed by a strange feeling flowing through me. I must have been affected by my spiritual trip to our Lady of Walsingham and I immediately thought of the biblical story of the good Samaritan. He too came across a traveller lying by the side of the road and stopped to help the injured man. However, I don't think the Good Samaritan played golf as I seemed to have little problem in leaving Big George stranded on the side of the road and set off by myself in order to get back in time.

I'm sure you will be glad to hear that I got back just in time to get to the first tee. I didn't hear from Big George and I was worried that if he blows up after only 50 miles then the 300-mile trip to Paris would be an even bigger challenge. On the positive side, I did at least now know that if we are in danger of missing our pre-booked train back from Paris I will have no problem leaving him on the side of the road, especially as he claims he can speak French.

Chapter 17
(Visits 7,897 only 42,103 to go)

After weeks of preparation the time had finally come for my Paris café cycle ride. I felt that to increase readership I needed a big event to spread word of the blog further. I hoped this one would take the blog to the next level.

As per all my rides it was spiced up by aiming to find the best cafe anywhere between London and Paris (which I happen to stop at). The ride was also the last chance for somewhere to become European cafe of the year. I had kept planning at a high level, the overnight accommodation was booked and route entered into my bicycle GPS but I was leaving the café stops to lady luck.

The one thing I didn't have any control over was how Big George would perform. I was worried that he had not done enough training for the punishing schedule, both in terms of miles and amount of coffee I required him to drink. I had last seen him on the side of the road nursing his knee so wasn't sure what state he would be in or even if he would turn up at Norwich Station ready to catch the evening train down to London.

After a nervous wait, I was pleased to see him wheel his bike down the platform and that he still appeared to be in one piece but as we loaded our bikes into the guards van and made our way to our seats it was obvious that there was an elephant in the carriage. After a few moments of rather stilted conversation Big George confessed that he had been thinking a lot about why he had performed so badly on our last ride and had prepared a list of six reasons which he wanted to go through.

First, he reckoned his brakes were rubbing making it harder to pedal. Then he thought his seat was too low, yada, yada, yada, yawn, yawn. I soon glazed over as he went through each item in detail but I did notice that he hadn't included on the list lack of training or the fact he needed to man up when suffering on the bike. Despite this I still appreciated the work that had gone into putting his excuses list together and it nicely broke the ice as we sped through the East Anglian countryside down to the big smoke.

The rest of the journey was spent studying my Avenue Verte route map guide-book. I was sure the book would be invaluable at estimating how long the various legs would take and I would also be able to bore Big George with interesting facts about the sights we would see on the way.

We pulled into Liverpool Street station on time and went to collect our bikes. I loaded the first route on to my GPS and we set off for our initial stop, the London Eye where the route officially started. Big George wanted to know why we were not going straight to the hotel and making this unnecessary detour. I explained that his ridiculous suggestion would mean missing out part of the official London to Paris (Avenue Verte) route, which I intended to follow meticulously. He had much to learn.

Riding in London is very different from the quiet country lanes that we were used to but at this time into the evening, the traffic wasn't particularly bad and we got to the London Eye in one piece. We took the requisite 'start of the London to Paris ride' photo. Disappointingly there was no plaque to mark the actual start point but my guide-book definitely said this was the right place so I decided to make the entrance to the London Eye the kick off for recording the mileage etc.

Now we were on the official route we could cycle the first official 10 miles (on the Avenue Verte) across London to our hotel. As this is an official bike route it insisted on going on every bit of available cycle path so we went along the Thames tow-path for a bit, on cycle paths marked on the road and wove in and out of local paths. It was certainly not the way the crow would fly but Tufty Squirrel would have given it the thumbs up for road safety. Because of this it took

90 mins to complete this short stretch, which was twice as long as I had planned and set a trend for the rest of the trip.

We spent the night at the Wandsworth Premier Inn. Big George had researched that the Premier Inn have a cycling friendly policy where they guarantee somewhere safe for your bike to be kept overnight or you can keep them in your room. Despite its proximity to the Avenue Verte the Premier Inn Wandsworth clearly didn't get many cyclists staying as the best they could come up with for safe bike storage was the mop cupboard. We squeezed the bikes in with the cleaning equipment and watched as the door was locked for the night.

As it was getting late we ate in the restaurant and retired for the night. I just had time to get out my precious route map guide-book and check out what we had in store for us the next day when we planned to cycle the 100 miles to the coast.

In the morning, we had a porridge-based breakfast at a local café and then returned to rescue our bikes from the cleaner's cupboard. I popped my pannier on to the bike and waited while Big George tied his travelling pack on to his back rack. It seemed a complicated procedure which I found amusing at first but increasingly frustrating as the trip wore on.

I soon realised my 15mph planning assumption was a bit ambitious as we averaged only 10mph through Greater London on a further series of stop start cycle paths. On the map, it had looked like cycle paths all the way out of London which I had assumed we could bomb along. But of course, there were lots of junctions and pelican crossings meaning that you could never get up to speed for any length of time.

I also discovered my idea of only having one pannier scored well on its primary weight saving function but made the bike very unstable. This was causing the back wheel to slide from beneath me on sharp corners and I soon fell off (I made a note on my learnings spreadsheet to take two panniers on any future trips). After a while I worked out how to keep my balance but it did slow us down.

Our progress was slowed even more when Big George got a puncture in the so-called puncture proof tyres I had lent him.

While he got to work changing the inner tube I thought I would check the route map guide-book to see how we were doing. I checked the special pannier pocket I had allocated for it but it wasn't there. I continued to search frantically unpacking the whole bag but there was no sign of it. To my horror, I realised I had left it in the hotel. This was not good: although we were mainly navigating off my Garmin Sat Nav, it did mean that with no route map guide book I no longer had any back up in case of GPS failure and the daily debrief would not be filled with useful facts read out of the book. When I told him, Big George didn't seem at all disappointed about missing out on this particular treat.

We had only covered 17 miles but as it had taken over two hours I decided it was time to get down to the main reason we were here, which was to find the best café anywhere between London and Paris. I suggested we stop at the next independent café or tearoom we came across. Which turned out to be Poppy's cafe in Coulson Park.

To date I had never found a good cafe in a park so expectations were low. I was pleased to see that the outside seating area had a lovely view of the park and it was also well shielded from the road. To my surprise the cake selection was very good and I gave a high ECS rating.

My cheese scone had been lightly grilled and was excellent especially as they had remembered the old rhyme "cheese scone hot, fruit scone not". Big George said his fruit cake was very good too. Our drinks were also both nice so we agreed Poppy's had set the London to Paris cafe bar high.

We were now out of London but things didn't improve, as we had to cycle over the North Downs. It was slow going up and due to my bike balance issue I was slow coming back down too. The views were stunning and for the first time we seemed to be in the country. This feeling didn't last long as we continued at snail's pace out towards Gatwick airport.

The cycle route goes through the airport and parallel to the runway. The airport people had sensibly separated the two with the use of a high fence to avoid cyclists mistakenly getting in the way of the planes but it was still quite exciting.

Today's ride was estimated at 94 miles and about 7 hours of riding but when we stopped for lunch we had taken 5 hours to do only 34 of those miles. I told Big George the bad news and with no map guide-book I didn't really know what terrain to expect. I said that we would need to put the hammer down a bit if we were going to get to Seaford before nightfall.

Big George suggested we should just grab a sandwich for lunch to make up some time. I reminded him our primary objective was to find the best café anywhere between London and Paris and this would not be achieved with a takeaway lunch. Judging by his reaction I'm not sure he was yet with the programme but I did persuade him to stop at the nearby Charlie's deli.

Big George was still in a sulk and ordered Thai chicken noodles before refusing to have any coffee and cake. This meant scores for Charlie's deli were incomplete but as my hot chocolate and red velvet cake were not as good as Poppy's I was happy we still had a clear leader.

Refuelled I hoped to get back on schedule but before we even got back on the bikes Big George threw another spanner in the works by announcing he was having a recurrence of the knee injury. As there were another 260 miles between here and Paris this didn't bode well for the trip let alone our chances of getting to tonight's accommodation.

It was time for my legendary motivational skills to come into play so I gave him some painkillers, told him to man up and set off down the road. This didn't seem to do the trick as he was still moaning a few miles later. Once again I was standing by Big George who was sitting on the side of the road massaging his knee. This time I needed him to be my cycling guest reviewer so, much as I wanted to, I couldn't leave him. I too suffer from an occasional dodgy right knee but I had sensibly brought my knee brace with me, which I was currently wearing. For the good of the trip I agreed to sacrifice it to give us any chance of making it to the ferry port.

We set off again and a combination of the knee brace, pain-killers and a good talking to seemed to settle his knee down enough to continue. My GPS was not impressed with our progress and was predicting that we wouldn't get to the hotel until well after dark.

Since Gatwick the route had mainly been on a series of flat if bumpy off-road cycle paths, first the Worth Way then the Forrest Way. The good news was that we could get up a bit of speed for long stretches, but I was glad I had chosen to bring my cyclo cross bike with its wide 28mm tyres as it felt as though we were riding in the Paris-Roubaix spring cycling monument race (not that I have).

As long as we could keep this pace up I was now confident of reaching Seaford in daylight. Nothing is ever that straightforward on a cycling adventure and I had not factored in the hills of the South Downs that we were required to cross next. Big George's bad knee and poor pre-trip training regime meant that as we started climbing the hills I soon got a long way ahead and Big George was left out of sight far behind me. At a village at the top of one particularly steep climb I even managed some shopping while I waited for him to turn up. Our average speed had once again dropped and the schedule was in tatters.

We required an emergency cafe stop so that Big George could refuel and take on the power of cake for the final 35-mile push. It was already 5:00pm and would be dark about 8:00pm. Luckily, we came across Forgewood camp-site cafe bar half way up a hill so despite the lateness of the day and the time it would take to have a rest we cycled in. On the plus side, it would mean I could check out another café on my search.

Once inside we discovered that the cafe bar had only scones and croissants but no cake so got a poor ECS rating and instantly out of the running for an award. It wasn't all bad news as croissants and jam are top energy food so we filled up on them plus hot chocolate and coffee.

Now Big George's fuel gauge was on full we were ready to set off again and as we left the South Downs behind we were able to pick up the pace as we hit the fantastic all tarmac, off road, cuckoo trail. It was now getting dark and as our lights were more for being seen by, rather than seeing with, we had to slow down for the last few miles, as we couldn't see the road surface properly.

We eventually pulled into our hotel in the pitch dark at 9:00pm after 97 miles and twelve hours riding. Big George was unhappy and tired so he only managed two pints in the bar, before we crashed out in our room. Overall, I felt it had been both a dramatic and successful day of cafe cycle reviewing. I had plenty of stuff to update the blog with so burnt the midnight oil to make sure my followers didn't miss out on the day's action (although judging by the viewing figures they did). I hoped readers' excitement would pick up as the journey unfolded on the French side.

Chapter 18
(Visits 7,907 only 42,043 to go)

The next morning I told Big George that I was expecting yesterday to have been the toughest day of this particular adventure but this proved to be far from the case.

I wasn't planning to be able to do any cycle cafe reviewing today as we would be on the ferry for most of the time and had then arranged to get to our overnight accommodation by 7:30pm. This would mean we would have to go flat out for 45 miles across France. To encourage Big George I said that if we weren't there on time we wouldn't get an evening meal. Although this was technically a lie I felt it was the correct motivational approach required for the occasion.

We left the White Lion in Seaford early to cycle the 3 miles to the ferry. I wanted to leave us enough time in order that: I could buy better lights for my bike, Big George could purchase a knee brace (so I could have mine back) and I could try and replace my map route guide book. We were successful on the first two but failed to source a replacement map route guide-book. (Later that day I did manage to pick up a leaflet about the route in the information section on the ferry, albeit in French and with only a tiny map, so not much of a replacement really.)

Catching the ferry was a remarkably straightforward process. After collecting our boarding passes we had to wait in the car park with a lot of other cyclists. By chatting with likeminded people, we soon realised we were not the only ones on the London to Paris trip. Obviously, we had to work out who was going the furthest and planning to be the quickest. We developed an approach of eavesdropping on all the conversations going on around us before comparing notes. From our analysis of the information we gleaned that we were planning to do the trip in the fewest days plus no one else seemed to be in search of the best café on the route clearly making us the most hardcore. Some of the other cyclists were planning to include something called sightseeing on their rides. I asked them what rating system they would be using to decide on the best site they would be seeing but apparently, it doesn't work like that. So not only does sightseeing slow you down but there is no winner. Very strange.

Once we had loaded our bikes on board ship we made our way to the seating area to settle down for the 4-hour crossing. There was no further ferry-based activity to report as we played I-Spy (mostly with things beginning with S) until we arrived in France and disembarked (ferry speak for got off) with our bikes. I quickly adjusted to riding on the right side of the road with a gentle reminder from the traffic heading straight for me on the road out of Dieppe. It was then on to 30 miles of tarmacked, off-road, pancake flat cycle path as we sped along enjoying the lovely French countryside. I was very impressed with the quality of the French cycle path but this stretch gave us rather high French cycle path expectations, which were never met again during the rest of the trip.

*****

We were making excellent progress and enjoying the track so much that we missed our turn off. Once I had corrected the error we had 15 miles and plenty of time to get to our stop by the 7:30pm dinner cut off. Unfortunately, this final stretch was rather hilly and as I had discovered the day before this was not Big George's strong point and we soon lost all the time we had made up.

We arrived at 7:40 and were greeted by the owners of Chambres d'hôtes "La Brayonne" Sophie and Erick. We would be the only guests that night and would be eating with our hosts once we had freshened up. I informed Big George that I had persuaded them to feed us but not to say anything.

As our accommodation was away from any town or village Big George was worried that he wouldn't be getting any beer tonight. His fears were short lived as Sophie provided a fantastic meal (including traditional French cheeses, or fromage) accompanied by homemade aperitif, homemade cider, red wine and calvadre (cider brandy). The whole lot was superb and just what we needed after our dash from the ferry.

Sophie spoke very good English and Big George a bit (petit) of French but I don't speak French nor Erick English. Everything was fine until Big George popped to the loo and Sophie had to answer the phone. This left me and poor Erik looking nervously at each other across the table until he wisely decided to go and cut some more bread in the kitchen. It's at times like this I wish I was better at languages, but they are all Dutch to me.

Once they returned we chatted away and Sophie asked what I did for a living. I explained that I was now retired but spent most of my time cycling to cafes to review their cakes and drinks. Sophie translated for Erick whose response to me was "N'avez-vous rien de mieux à faire avec votre temps?" (Haven't you got anything better to do with your time?)

We had a great evening and it was nice to be able to talk with some real people and not just hotel reception staff and café baristas. As it was getting late we went off to bed to rest up before tomorrow's 'big day' - we needed to ride 100 plus miles without the aid of a map route guide book.

Before going to bed each night, I made sure I posted that day's adventure in the hope that it might attract a bigger audience but in fact my viewing figures were dwindling.

*****

Sophie had prepared us a super breakfast of fresh eggs from her chickens and a selection of homemade breads and jams. Before we left she gave us some emergency bread as she could obviously tell we were the type of cyclists likely to need it.

With an early start under our belts we quickly conquered the Normandy hills, making good progress as most of France seemed to still be in bed. Big George started to tell me some stories about when he had cycled in these parts many years ago. He kept apologising in case I had heard these tales before. I explained to him that I didn't actually listen to any of his stories (or anything he said), so he was free to tell them to me as often as he liked, which he did.

By mid-morning we were in need of refuelling and on the lookout for a cafe stop. It may have been because it was a Saturday or because it was August but France appeared to be shut and we couldn't find anywhere for refreshments. I was a bit disappointed when the only option we could find was in the centre of the large city of Beauvais, by the cathedral.

The cafe was called Le Zinc Bleu (The blue Zinc) and was fairly basic. Back in England I have been to many cafes that put a few tables and chairs on the pavement in an attempt to create a continental feel. So I was looking forward to seeing a real pavement set up. However, on a cold and drizzly day our French hosts clearly couldn't be bothered as the outdoor seating area was packed away. This would never happen at home as whatever the weather if a café has a pavement seating facility they will put it out despite there being no prospect of anyone using it.

We went inside to the only seats available. I asked if they had gateaux (which I believe is French for cake) but they only did croissant, baguette and jam. This was not how I had pictured things. We had no choice but to order bread and jam with hot chocolate for me and coffee for Big George.

It was all nice enough but certainly did nothing to threaten the Hotel Vitranic in Slovenia who continued to be placed at the top of the European cafe of the year leader board or Poppy's as the best cafe between London and Paris (which I happen to stop at).

I did have a second reason for suggesting we stop here as I had noticed that next door was the tourist information centre. This could be the opportunity to replace my route map guide book. I went in waving the London to Paris bike ride leaflet that I got off the ferry yesterday and asked if they had the full guide. With much mutual excitement, (hoorays and oh la la's) they whipped out the very book I was after. I grabbed it with glee and quickly started to thumb through but soon noticed that the words made no sense, I deduced that this must be what French looks like. I asked if they had it in English but 'non' ('no').

By now Big George had finished his petit dejeuner but had made a café stop school-boy error (CSSBE). He still hadn't noticed his mistake as we set off again to find the route starting to flatten out. I was therefore surprised when a few miles later Big George announced he was almost out of water and needed a drink. His CSSBE had been not to refill his water bottle at our earlier café stop. I on the other hand still had a full one. As a team player, I kindly offered to sell Big George some of mine at an appropriately inflated price. This would not only help to rehydrate him but give him a useful lesson on market forces as well. He politely declined my selfless offer.

Big George struggled on until, further down the road, we were stopped and asked to complete a census about the Euro Velo cycle network. It seemed rude not to. We were handed clip-boards, question sheet and pens. I randomly ticked some boxes on the English version of the form, which seemed to make the census man very happy. As a reward, we were given a short talk about the Euro Velo network. It turned out that we were currently cycling on route 2, which goes from Oslo to Spain. To tempt us further he then showed us a map of where all 15 routes go and I got very excited to see London to Rome was one of them. There would be plenty of café reviewing possibilities on that ride I thought. Big George didn't seem to share my excitement instead he asked the census man if he knew where he could get some water, but he didn't nor did another French cyclist standing with us also randomly ticking away. The talk of water had made me thirsty so I had a nice large gulp from my bottle obviously forcing the price of my water to go up again.

As we continued on our way I started to notice another phenomenon in these parts. It appears that in France they think it is a good idea to build all their towns at the top of step hills and the joker who put together the Avenue Verte route thought it would be funny to keep getting cyclists to ride to the top of them.

When the joke was played for the third time we had had enough and decided to stop for our lunch at the top of Claremont. I later discovered that there is a plan to build a flatter version of Avenue Verte on a purpose-built path, which would avoid all the ups and downs but this was no help to us today.

As France continued to still be mainly shut we had to do with a takeaway picnic style lunch with items brought from the patisserie (cake shop) and delicatessen (delicatessen). Buying your cake from a dedicated shop meant the effective cake selection rating would be very high although you may recall this isn't a factor in the European café rating system so didn't help the rating on this occasion.

We ate our food on benches at the top of the town hill but the overall experience didn't score that highly, especially as we couldn't get any take away hot drinks, although Big George did get water.

We now hit some good bits of cycle track interspersed with parts going through towns and villages on busy roads. It was becoming a long afternoon of stop start cycling. At one point, we found our route blocked as there was a local bike race doing circuits around the village. The marshals wouldn't let us continue our journey until the cyclists had come around with a gap big enough for us to get back on our way. By now the race had broken up into several groups and no gaps seemed to be forth coming. It looked like we would be stuck for a long time, which was a problem as the clock was ticking and we still had many miles to go. I decided to hatch a cunning plan. The next time a group came past we would leap on our bikes and pretend we were in the race until we got to our turning at which point we would veer off and be on our way.

We found a space between marshals and as the next group approached we hopped on board and tucked in at the back. This seemed to work well but we quickly realised it was a fading group and soon found ourselves at the front of the pack and closing in on the main peloton.

It was clear that these were not actually very good local village cyclists as even with my pannier and off-road tyres I was in danger of catching them up and taking the lead. Although I was tempted to go all out for the win, our route turned off at the next corner and I reluctantly let them go.

After we left the race the route went up a very steep (and I mean very steep) hill to the start of a long section through some woods. I promised I would not put in the blog the picture I took of Big George having to get off and push his bike up and, as a good cycling host, I didn't use it, although I did post a good one of him getting off just about to start pushing.

At the top of the hill we discovered the best section of the ride that day: a trail through some woods which went on for several miles before going past the impressive Chateau de Chantilly and Chantilly race course. I only discovered where this was when later researching for the day's post. At the time, I told Big George it must be the Palace of Versailles (Buckingham Palace) and he was suitably impressed by my knowledge of posh French buildings. It wasn't long after this that we got into the next town, Senlis. Due to the previous long traffic-free section we had made up some time. It was now 4:30 and sunset was in just over 3 hours meaning that with only 30 of our 105 miles left we would have plenty of time to take a cafe break.

Big George explained to me that French people get their cake from the cake shop (patisserie) and take it with them to eat at the cafe bar. This seemed a good system as you always get a good cake selection but does make it difficult to know if you are rating one establishment or two. I checked my café cycle review book, which clearly stated that it is only the café where you consumed your food and drink that will be rated. We split into two groups so while I got the cake from the nearby patisserie (cake shop), Big George sorted out coffee and hot chocolate at cafe le Balto.

Cafe Balto seemed typically French but, sitting outside, neither of us liked the amount of smoking going on around us. Our drinks were at the better end of the spectrum both being strong and hot. Not surprisingly the cakes I had purchased were very good, but overall the whole package did not do enough to win either of the current best cafe prizes.

My suspicions about the last leg of today's ride were first raised when the route signs turned off the smooth cycle path and across an overgrown field down to the river. The Avenue Verte signs were overgrown so I suspected that this was not the way the locals came but without a map we had no alternative other than to continue this way. I wrongly assumed that when we reached the river it would then turn back into a nice concrete tow-path but once at the water it turned out to be an even worse slippery mud track. We battled on across this terrain for several miles until it returned to proper roads.

Progress had been painfully slow and it was now getting dark. I was glad that I had upgraded my bike lights the day before and patted myself on the back. The lack of daylight made finding the hotel more difficult than it needed to be but we got there in the end and reported to reception. Once again, the only place for our bikes was the broom cupboard where they were locked away for the night.

The hotel I had booked was a posh French 4-star job, which I had got on a special deal on the internet. Because it was late and we were tired we opted to eat in the hotel restaurant.

When we sat down the sniffy waiters brought us menus, which were all in French. Luckily, one of them spoke English and translated for us but it was all expensive fancy French style stuff. What we really wanted was a double cheese-burger and chips but had to make do with the Saturday night set menu. It was very tasty but the portions were tiny so I was still rather hungry when I had finished the meal. This was clearly an emergency food situation so on returning to the room I unwrapped the package containing the emergency bread that Sophie had so wisely given us that morning.

Chapter 19
(Visits 8,004 only 41,996 to go)

The final part of our London to Paris ride would be a 50-mile section with a finish at Notre Dame cathedral. From there it would be a short ride to the Gare du Nord (North Station) to catch the Eurostar train home. It is always important to have some jeopardy so I had made sure we had a deadline for today's finale. Our bikes had to be delivered to the Eurostar luggage area by 3:15 pm or they would not be on the train with us back to London and we would therefore not be able to get to our train back to Norwich. To make sure there would be no slip ups we went for breakfast at 7:30 giving us plenty of time to get to Paris on schedule.

At our posh French hotel, the breakfast was a very expensive buffet style affair. With no emergency bread left I decided to go to the restaurant in my cycle top so I could stuff croissants and pastries into its many pockets. We could then eat for free if we had any more emergency food situations later in the day.

I had stolen food from many a hotel breakfast buffet but today I hit an unexpected problem. At such an early time on a Sunday morning all the other guests were still in bed. This meant we were the only guests in the restaurant and therefore nicking pastries would be far more challenging than expected. As we sat at our table we hatched a plan.

I walked confidently back to the buffet area and waited as Big George summoned the waiters and started to chat to them in his best pigeon French (francais de pigeon). While the waiters tried to decipher his French/Scottish mumblings I managed to snaffle 4 mini croissants, 3 mini choc au pain and 2 mini pain au raisins into my cycle jacket pouches before backing out of the restaurant while Big George pretended to choke on his baguette.

Before we were rumbled we quickly retrieved our bikes from the broom cupboard and checked out. It was then a fast pedal from the hotel back to the safety of the official route. The first part of today's ride was excellent, as we rode along the side of the river Oise, then through some woods before following the banks of the famous river Seine (Thames). All of it along purpose built, traffic free, cycle track.

Everything was going smoothly so in relaxed mood we decided to play a game called 'who can name the most famous French people'. The idea of the game is to take it in turns to name a famous French person (including a short summary of why they were famous). Whoever names the most famous French people wins. Our version of the game didn't last very long as I only came up with four and lost as Big George just reeled off a series of so called famous French rugby players. My four were: Louis Pasture (who invented milk), Louis 14th (who is the king of France), Asterix the Gaul (who defeated the Romans) and his son Charles de Gaul (who built an airport). I made a note to do some more famous French people research ready for next time I play this game.

With only 18 miles to go and apparently plenty of time left we decided to stop at Bistro se Mamie for a leisurely mid-morning break and café review. Would this be the one? (It wasn't). It did start well as we reclined into a pleasant outside seating area overlooking the river.

As they had no cake I got out the emergency pastries from breakfast and ate a complete set. In terms of drinks Big George thought his coffee was a bit weak but, although not spectacular, I found my hot chocolate to be the best one I had had in France. Despite this the Bistro se Mamie would not be winning anything on this showing.

With time in hand we quickly covered several more miles on good quality tow-paths. There was even time to start planning our Paris sight-seeing tour in the extra couple of hours we would have before departure. But there is many a slip between cup and lip (beaucoup loin de la coupe aux levres) as we hit the suburbs of Paris.

One thing that had particularly impressed me about the Avenue Verte was the clear signposting. Other than central London you could pretty much do the route by just following the signs. This had made navigation straight-forward and combined with my Garmin we hardly missed a turn or made a navigational blunder. However, as soon as we entered Greater Paris the excellent route signage all but disappeared and I now had to navigate just from my GPS, a basic system, which is good on the open road but less good in an urban area.

With faltering progress the time started to slip by while the miles passed slowly. Panic started to set in but we pressed on and re-enacted the final stage of the tour de France with a sprint finish along the streets of central Paris, arriving at Notre Dame with our sight-seeing plans in ruins.

We only had time to grab a quick photo of each of us standing in front of the cathedral before heading off to find the Gare du Nord .

Getting there was easy but all the signs at the station were in French so it took some time to find where our bikes needed to go before a final dash down a platform.

The man in the luggage office took our booking forms and congratulated me on a successful trip before saying we had just made it with only a few minutes to spare. Actually, he could have been saying anything as it was in French but I like to think this is what he meant.

I was very pleased with my planning. We had done a 350-mile ride before arriving at our destination within 5 minutes of the deadline. Pretty damn good estimating skills I thought, well done me (bien me faire).

With bikes safely delivered we had a 90 -minute wait before our train was due to depart. Much to Big George's delight, I announced that there was just enough time for one last cycle cafe review at one of the cafes across the road from the Gare du Nord . We choose cafe Au Rendezvous des Belges (meeting with Belgiums, although we didn't).

Surprisingly, for such a tourist trap it was the best cafe stop we went to in France, partly because we could relax having achieved our goal and partly because the hot drinks, beer and food (plus the remaining emergency breakfast food) all hit the spot.

Big George voted it our best cafe stop but I still felt (and was backed up by the numbers) that Poppy's was the winner of the best cafe between London and Paris (which I happened to stop at) so when I got back home I made them a certificate which they were very excited to receive.

The return to Norwich turned out to be plain sailing from the point we boarded the train to arriving safely back home.

We agreed that the official London to Paris cycle route on Avenue Verte had been very good in some places and very disappointing in others. I collected our feedback forms, although only one had been filled in, and after reviewing the input I was able to declare it as an officially successful trip.

I also wrote a factual description of the route for the blog with added maps and included some top tips. I was hoping it might attract a few views but soon, and rather disappointingly, it became my most read post showing that people probably just wanted facts and reviews rather than the café based waffle I included in my normal posts.

It was time to take stock. The blog was still attracting a steady if not growing following but still at a rate where I would lose my bet to Barry by several years. It was clearly time to get back on track and take the calorie neutral cafe cycle ride off the back burner as my best chance for success.

Chapter 20
(Visits 8,805 only 41,195 to go)

It had been quite a while since my brother Duncan had challenged me to demonstrate how encouraging people to eat cake could help solve the UK's obesity crisis. I planned to prove the point by setting the world record for a calorie neutral bike ride and had not been put off by the setbacks encountered (first the Guinness Book of World Records refused to validate this activity and then I had my NDE).

Since the Guinness Book of so called World Records washed their hands of me I now considered myself the self-appointed arbiter of the record. With such a role comes responsibilities, the first of which was to come up with the rules by which to govern any attempt. It took many long minutes but I eventually came up with the following.

1. The holder of the record will have visited the highest number of different cafes during a single day.
2. All cafes must be independent and not part of national chains.
3. All cafes must be visited within their normal opening hours and not open early or kept opened late especially for the record attempt.
4. At each cafe a standard portion of cake or a scone (fruit or cheese) must be consumed. Biscuits, flapjacks or anything pre-packaged will not count.
5. At each cafe a hot chocolate must be consumed.
6. From the time of arriving at the cafe 400 calories must be burnt before the next cafe can be visited thus making the ride calorie neutral. (400 calories are based on in-depth internet research on average calories of cakes or scones plus those of a typical hot chocolate).
7. If extra calories have been used between cafes then this is tough, as they cannot be credited against other legs of the ride.

Rule 6 proved to be my most controversial rule as many people were adamant that a cake and hot chocolate contained more than 400 calories. However, I went to several on-line sites (two to be precise) that gave calories for different food types. I averaged out standard cake and scone portion calories and it came to 220 calories for cake and 180 for hot chocolate and as official arbiter for the record that was good enough for me.

With everything in place, I planned a five-stop trip visiting some of my favourite cafes. I wanted to see what I could learn about high speed cafe cycling and also to set what I believed would be a challenging number of cafes for an acceptable world record.

*****

I was fortunate that the day I picked had perfect weather with warm sun and a light breeze. I skipped my breakfast, to start the day on zero calories, and at 8.30 I set off for my first destination, the Box Tree cafe in Brooke.

On arrival, I noticed that the cafe had changed its name from the Box Tree Cafe to just The Cafe. Whilst ordering my hot chocolate and orange cake, I enquired as to the reason for the name change. Apparently, a rival Box Tree restaurant in Sheffield had bagged naming rights and written to all other Box Trees to tell them to change their names. Although this seemed a little harsh, the Brooke version felt it easier to change their name rather than fight back. I promised I would update my blog with the new name, as I didn't want to be held responsible for anyone setting off for a short ride to Brooke and ending up in South Yorkshire.

I sat down with my first drink and cake to try and consume them as quickly as possible. The hot chocolate was very hot, which normally I approve of, but made it hard to drink as quickly as I would have liked.

I checked my calorie counting watch and noted that I had burnt 34 calories whilst at the Cafe. What a bonus! I hadn't taken the cake eating calorie burn into account in my original planning. It meant I would have calories in hand for the rest of the ride, although rule 7 makes it clear that this will not give me an advantage.

I left The Cafe in Brooke, and headed off to the Hen House near Wymondham for my next stop. On arrival, I checked that enough calories had been burnt (they had) and headed straight to the counter to get my next energy refill. On this occasion, I had a cheese scone to accompany my hot chocolate.

I took the opportunity to ask if Annabel, the owner, knew the calorie content of the drink and scone to help validate my research. She didn't but appeared to be a bit of a calorie expert and was more than happy to perform some energy estimating. Her conclusion was that it would be about 180 for the hot chocolate. She proudly explained that it came from Holland (fortunately not Chocomel) although it wasn't clear if Dutch calories are the same as British ones. She reckoned that it would be 200 calories for scone plus butter. This was good as I now had a self-proclaimed calorie expert to quote if anyone challenged my calculations.

While I waited for my hot chocolate to cool I got side-tracked discussing saddle comfort options with some fellow cyclists who were admiring my bike. When I checked my watch, I was way behind schedule. I made a note to not get involved in idle chit-chat on the official attempt and stay focused on the matter in hand.

The next stop was a ride up to Mattishall, and Tabnabs. On arrival, I was very pleased to hear from Mrs Tabnabs that she had had several cyclists visit her after reading the recommendation from my blog. Maybe I was becoming an internet sensation after all.

To continue my calorie research, I asked the staff if they had any idea on calorie content but unfortunately no one in the cafe could help. Without any calorie portion guidance, I opted for a large slice of peanut cake. Trying to drink the excellent thick and very hot hot chocolate quickly proved challenging but with the clock ticking I finished it before (with a burnt mouth) setting off for Reepham.

I decided to go to Reepham railway station as on my last visit there I had had a very tasty and infeasibly large cheese scone which I really fancied again.

I ordered the cheese scone and indeed it was still infeasibly large. I accompanied it with yet another hot chocolate. The scone was great but I really didn't want a fourth hot chocolate. There was nothing wrong with it, in fact it was a very nice drink and I did eventually work my way through it, however I knew I could not face any more hot chocolate today.

This was bad as if I could only manage 4 or 5 cafes before being sick it wouldn't be a very impressive record. There is one big advantage of being the self-appointed arbiter of a world record in that you are at liberty to change the rules, so in order to make things lighter on the stomach I revisited rules 5 and 6. They would now include the option for other hot beverages and not just hot chocolate. An added advantage of this would be reducing the number of calories to burn between cafes as, according to further in-depth internet research, there are far fewer calories in white tea and coffee (no sugar) than hot chocolate. Therefore rules 5 and 6 were amended to:

5. At each cafe a standard hot drink must be consumed. (Tea, coffee or hot chocolate)
6. From the time of arriving at the cafe 300 calories must be burnt before the next cafe can be visited thus making the ride calorie neutral. (300 calories are based on in-depth internet research on average calories of cakes and scones plus average calories of a hot drink (Tea, coffee, hot chocolate).

With the new rules in place it was back to Norwich and my local cafe; Stephanie's in Eaton. Here I went for tea and blueberry muffin. The tea was great and refreshing and I manged two cups which settled my stomach down.

I got home to study the data (which I posted for other cycle calorie data buffs to enjoy) and work out what would be a challenging cafe target for next year's world record attempt. Today's learnings needed to be incorporated into my next trial run, planned for the spring, before tackling the big one next summer.

I still needed to visit more cafes and tearooms to give me enough options to plan my route so there would be no let-up in my search and reviewing of new venues, but after the trial run I felt the calorie neutral bike ride world record was back on track.

The same couldn't be said in terms of becoming an internet sensation. I was approaching 10,000 visits to my blog but this would not satisfy Barry.

Chapter 21
(Visits 10,429 only 39,671 to go)

As Summer turned to Autumn I struggled to come up with new ideas to move the blog on to the next rung of the internet sensation ladder. Then a light bulb went on during my next ride with Big George.

As always, Big George turned up to the start of the ride with a logistical constraint. This time it was a last-minute dentist appointment, meaning we would only have time for a morning ride. Luckily, I had recently noticed a new cafe, called Every Day's a Picnic (EDAP), not too far away so this seemed an ideal opportunity to check it out.

After an hour or so of riding and reminiscing we arrived at EDAP's well-presented outdoor seating courtyard area where we parked our bikes before going inside to check out the cakes. The staff were very friendly and I was extremely pleased when they seemed to know all about my blog and had even forwarded one of my posts to a biking friend of theirs.

Big George was clearly itching to join in and didn't want to miss out on the conversation. He could contain himself no longer and leapt forward to introduce himself. 'I'm Big George' he said, 'and I'm often the star of the blog'. After much Big George-led blog chat I reminded him of our time constraint and was eventually able to get us back on the job in hand, the café cycle review.

We checked out the cakes and ordered our drinks. The problem was that now Big George thought he was a celebrity he felt he no longer had to pander to my cafe reviewing needs and instead of ordering a cake he went for a bacon ciabatta, thus rendering himself useless as a café reviewer.

We sat outside where Big George wanted to know if the other patrons wanted his autograph (they didn't).

On the route back, I tried to arrange a date for our next ride but he only wanted to discuss image rights and his new 'Big George' merchandise range. He made it clear that in future I was only to deal with him through his agent and he set off for the dentist, I assumed to have his teeth whitened.

As I wrote up the post, I started to think about where real cycling celebrities go on their rides. I realised it was a great opportunity to start a new blog feature called "celebrity cyclist X recommends...."

I went through my contacts list but discovered that I didn't actual know any celebrities, let alone cycling ones. Instead, I came up with a short target list of known celebrities who cycled or cyclists who were now celebrities. I went for Boris Johnson, Alan Sugar and former ironwoman triathlon world record holder Chrissie Wellington (from Norfolk). They each had a web site with a contact page so I sent them all a message telling them about the blog and asking them to let me know where their favourite café stop was when out cycling.

*****

While I waited for replies I had another event to take care of. It had now been a year since I started the blog. I had had 11,500 visits in the first year which was an average of 31 a day. I did the sums and worked out I would now need over 100 visits a day from now on to win the bet.

I couldn't let the blog's first birthday pass quietly so it was time for a 1st anniversary café cycle ride. It seemed the right thing to do was to take with me my first ever guest, Andrew (who has remained notoriously hard to please).

Andrew arrived on time but without an anniversary card, which I thought was very bad form even if I had forgotten to tell him it was a special anniversary ride. Due to the fog we took some time deciding on clothing layers. I sensibly went for short and Andrew foolishly went long and regretted this when the sun came out later in the ride.

For the first hour the fog and mist restricted the view and we could have been riding anywhere in the world (that was having a foggy day). After that the sun came out and with my legs at the perfect temperature we made it to the Dutch Barn Coffee shop which is at the Dutch Barn Nurseries in South Norfolk and not in Holland as you may have suspected.

We headed inside to check out the cakes. I chose chocolate and orange anniversary cake and Andrew chose carrot anniversary cake. Once again, I was disappointed that Andrew had not brought with him any candles for the cakes, or party hats. He had turned out to be a very poor choice for a special anniversary ride party guest indeed.

We decided to make the most of the nice autumn weather and sit at one of the tables spread amongst the garden centre plants. To avoid confusion, we sat well away from the garden gnomes.

The cakes and drinks arrived and looked very good. The one downside was that the cake had been placed on the serviette, rendering it useless for crumb removal purposes. Last time I had come across this practice I had decided to start a campaign to try and stamp it out and although I hadn't got around to doing anything about it yet, it was obviously going very well as this was the first time I had had the serviette ruined in this way for several months

Although not part of my ratings system we also had anniversary toasties. I was enjoying mine when Andrew asked me if I knew what really annoys him. I said yes I did, because I had kept a long list of them on my 'all the things Andrew has told me that really annoy him' spreadsheet on my phone. On this occasion, it turned out to be grapes in the garnish as he believes there is no place for fruit in salad, unless it's a fruit salad. I said I was already aware of this from when we had raisins in the coleslaw on our last ride so I updated the 'fruit in salad' count on the spreadsheet to two.

At the end of the ride I took the opportunity to look at some other stats and discovered I had now reviewed 57 local cafes plus another 18 in Europe. Considering my time out for the NDE it seemed a reasonable number but I was sure I could do a lot better in year two when hopefully I would finally become an internet sensation.

*****

To kick off my second year I came up with my second new idea. During rides, I had often noticed many houses and small farms selling eggs and other garden produce via an honesty table at the bottom of their drives. I realised that if I tracked the produce table contents and prices it would give me the opportunity to gather and pass on this useful information. I could share my findings as to where particularly good value eggs or unusual garden produce were available. I would start to include this new service in future posts. It would be called "Egg News" and I was sure that it would be both useful and informative for anyone needing half a dozen eggs, a fresh courgette or home-made strawberry jam (which is pretty much everybody).

Once word of Egg News spread I was sure this would attract lots of new readers and send my viewing figures spiralling up.

As this was very much a feature aimed at country day-trippers then what better ride to try this out on than a ride to the daddy of country day trips, a National Trust property.

This time I decided to take Big George as a safe café cycle bet.

Normally it is Andrew (who is notoriously hard to please) who spends our rides ranting about anything that doesn't align with his wishy washy liberal old person values so I was somewhat taken aback when I innocently asked Big George if he had seen yesterday's edition of the Great British Bake Off, only for it to lead to a passionate monologue-style rant about what was wrong with this country. Apparently too many men were watching Bake Off instead of doing more traditionally manly things like drinking beer and playing rugby. This was breaking down the traditional barriers of society leading to national chaos. "Before you know it some bloke will be posting pictures of cake on a blog", he said.

He made some good points but as a fan of Bake Off I couldn't agree so to avoid further conflict and make for a harmonious ride I decided to change the subject. I asked him if he had managed to complete the hoovering before the start of today's ride. His eyes lit up as he told me he had made a good start but still had got the stair carpet to do. He was confident of finishing it before Mrs Big George's weekly dust inspection.

We continued to discuss similarly urgent matters of the day as the miles zoomed past and we soon arrived at the Muddy Boots cafe in the car park at Blickling Hall, which to my relief was open this time. I was expecting a high standard to be set, starting with the cake selection, so we headed straight inside to see what was on offer.

As a National Trust staple I tried the cheese scone but could only describe it as 'fine' especially as it had not been warmed up and this was the cold cheese scone that broke the camel's back. I needed to up my game to get all cafes to warm up their cheese scones especially after the success of #keepcakeoffserviettes campaign. To make matters worse it was served on a paper plate which is only one up from a serviette.

On the return ride, it was time to concentrate on my new Egg News feature. It was a good route for eggs as just outside Hevingham we found eggs for sale at the knock down price of £1.00 a dozen. Assuming you could have half a dozen for 50p this made them by far the cheapest I had found anywhere. However, on closer inspection there were no eggs left in the egg box so I don't know if they had eggs or if it is just a marketing ploy to tempt you to buy the potatoes and onions that they did have. Very cunning these country folks.

A little further on we came to the small village of Tuttingham (pop. 8) where there appeared to be an egg price war. First, we saw eggs at 80p per half dozen which was obviously a clear attempt to undercut the eggs at £1.00 for half dozen eggs just a few yards down the road.

The rest of the ride went smoothly giving Big George ample time to finish his housework when he got home.

There was no time for me to get involved in my own household duties as I needed to get the blog up to date, share egg news and plan the next year of cycling and cake-based activity. At first the second year of blog viewings had started impressively with my best ever single day getting an unheard of 350 visits. Maybe it was Egg news, and with 100 visits over each of the next three days I thought maybe I had cracked it. At this rate, I would hit my target by the end of year two after all. Sadly, as quickly as the count had inexplicably gone up it returned to its normal low level.

Before I could get disheartened I received a reply from top triathlete Chrissie Wellington about my celebrity cyclist X recommends feature. She had kindly sent me the details of her favourite café cycle ride so at least that feature was up and running.

Chapter 22
(Visits 12,576 only 37,424 to go)

As a former triathlon champion (2013 Fritton lake Olympic distance male over 50s winner, beating four other old blokes to the title) I was really excited that fellow triathlon champion (4 times world Ironwoman champion) Chrissie Wellington had been the first celebrity to let me have their recommended favourite Tea Room and associated route. Chrissie Wellington was brought up in Norfolk and her chosen ride and café only needed a short train journey to reach so I arranged with Andrew to meet at Norwich station.

Chrissie had suggested a 62-mile cycle loop via Castle Acre and recommended the Church Gate Tea Room. This would be a long ride for us but a pre-breakfast warm up for her.

The train journey was uneventful allowing Andrew to list the topics he expected to be ranting about during the day. It was quite a long list as he had recently got back from a short break up North. To prove he was taking the ride seriously he had also been swotting up on our ride sponsor and would be sharing his top ten Chrissie Wellington facts throughout the day.

We alighted the train at Brandon and with the sky becoming more threatening we set off towards the start of the route at Feltwell (where Chrissie grew up, fact number 4).

Andrew was surprisingly positive as he announced how much he was enjoying the first proper winter ride of the year. He liked getting into his warm weather gear, he liked being on his steel winter bike and he liked the crispness in the air. Five minutes later the heavens opened and we were treated to some seriously heavy rain. Soaked and very cold, Andrew asked if his previous comments about winter cycling could be withdrawn.

To cheer us up Andrew shared Chrissie Wellington fact 8 (she is the same height as Tom Cruise) and fact 3 (she got an MBE in 2010 and has met the Queen, probably) before ranting about UHT milk in hotel rooms. With all the quality ranting and fact sharing the time flew by and we were soon at the Church Gate Tea room, Castle Acre. Just as the rain stopped.

The Church Gate Tea Room was coincidently next to the gate of Castle Acre church (what are the chances) and provided an outside seating area facility. As it was still a bit damp, and we were very wet, we choose to sit indoors where there was a lovely fire.

After examining and rating the ECS, I chose the chocolate cake to have with my hot chocolate and Andrew went for English Breakfast tea but then asked for cheese on toast (on brown). As cheese on toast (on brown) is clearly not cake he was not allowed to take part in any further cake based reviewing, which was rather disappointing on such a momentous ride.

My hot chocolate was very good as was Andrew's tea, but as per café rating rules there is a guest drink rating ceiling of 7 on a cup of tea as at the end of the day it is just a cup of tea.

Apart from our soaking the ride was going very well and the recommended tearoom was performing excellently but then I heard the email beep on my phone and things got even better.

Despite it being rude to check your phone at the table I needed to be distracted from Andrew's current rant on the poor quality of vegetarian pies up North as I had started to glaze over. I looked in my inbox to find the latest entry was from Boris Johnson (or at least his people) wanting to speak to me (or my people) in response to my request for a celebrity cyclist recommends suggestion but for now I had another celebrity ride to concentrate on.

Chrissie's recommendation of the Church Gate Tea Room had proved to be a very good one and went high up on my cafe league table, although shortly after our visit it closed down.

Before we left Andrew shared Chrissie Wellington fact 5, (she has been to Hawaii at least 4 times) and ranted about the pointlessness of flat caps in the 21st century.

We set off again in cold but dry conditions. Due to the fast, straight roads and with wind behind we got back to Brandon station in plenty of time for our train. Andrew was able to have a good rant about the afterlife while we waited for it to arrive (the train not the afterlife).

Andrew and I agreed that the ride was a great success so it was a big thank you to Chrissie (who has a degree in geography so can probably name all the capital cities of Europe, fact 7) for providing the route and excellent tea room recommendation. I was hoping that once some more Celebrity Cyclists had read the blog they would contact me with their recommendations (they didn't).

*****

I wanted to keep up the momentum from having my first celebrity on board so as soon as I got home, and posted about the ride, I did some more in-depth internet research about how to become a celebrity and discovered that it was important to have a presence on Twitter if you were really going to make it big.

I now had an excellent 3-point plan and once implemented was confident of success
1. Celebrity cyclist recommended rides
2. Egg News
3. Increase Social Media usage

I decided to focus on point three for now. Up until this point I had set up my blog under the name Norfolk Café Cycle Tour, which I had soon realised wasn't a very catchy name. Going on to Twitter gave me the chance for a bit of rebranding, which is how I became The Cake Crusader.

I excitedly sent my first tweet as the Cake Crusader, and the next day I got my first follower who turned out to be the other big name in café reviewing in the Norfolk area: The Fry Up Inspector.

Next, I raised my game by making a certificate for the winner of the European Café of the year with my colouring set. I scanned it and emailed it off to the Hotel Vitranc in Slovenia with a note of explanation in both English and a Google-translated Slovenian version. I was sure they would be both pleased and excited to receive it and I had asked them if they could send me a photo of them with the certificate. Much to my disappointment I did not receive a reply. It could only be because they were holding back until they had got press and TV coverage lined up.

Back on Twitter I was getting some steady growth – by the end of the week I had four followers. I tweeted some important café cycle news and tips but without a single retweet or any noticeable increase in visits to the blog.

Twitter wasn't proving to be the silver bullet I was hoping for. I decided to move Egg News on to Twitter. This would have two advantages. Firstly, it would not clog up the posts and second it would give those interested immediate news of egg availability and prices and if that didn't attract many more follows than nothing would.

It was still important to keep adding to the post count but I was surprised when Barry had asked if he could come along on the next ride. Up to this point he had showed little or no encouragement and certainly never read a post about my cycling adventures. Maybe he had had a change of heart and was going to confess that he could now see that people really did want to read about my cycling and cake based activities.

We were joined by Dom, a newbie cycling guest. There are three things you need to know about Dom.

1. I had known him for many years since we used to play cricket together in our youth
2. He is an old-school cyclist and doesn't like GPS or cycling computers
3. He is a self-proclaimed expert on Wales

Apart from the odd Christmas card we had not seen each other for many years until I recently received an email from him via the blog. He had been browsing the internet and come across one of my posts. Seeing my face outside one of his favourite cafes had taken him by surprise and as a fellow cyclist had inspired him to get in touch. Something he would later regret as he found himself walking his bike up another steep hill in Wales.

True to form Barry turned up with no Lycra, panniers on his hybrid bike and with hi viz cycle clips. This was not the attire or cycling kit I expected on my rides and was obviously another one of Barry's little digs at the foolishness of my cycling approach. Although Dom had turned up with the proper dress and kit I wasn't sure how well this ride would go.

Dom was showing a worrying care-free attitude. As an old-school cyclist, he had no discernible gadget to record the distance we covered, average speed of trip etc. I was confused as to what approach he took to fill in his cycling stats spreadsheet and produce his monthly cycling summary report (as I do). He explained that old-school cyclists did none of these things and just enjoyed going out for a ride. Very strange.

We arrived at our café to find Barry up to his old tricks. The café had listed the cakes available on a cake menu mini blackboard about the size of a computer tablet. Dom and I chose our cakes but Barry ordered a sausage sandwich. As a sausage sandwich is clearly not a cake (or listed on the cake menu mini blackboard) - he would take no further part in any cake related rating today although he didn't seem overly concerned.

When the cakes and drinks arrived, I tried to facilitate the critical activity of cafe cycle rating. Barry wouldn't rate his coffee as it was too hot and Dom said, 'well it's just cake isn't it' when I asked for his opinion. It was clear Barry's influence was spreading and he had only come along to sabotage the chances of me getting a new café cycling convert. I vowed to make sure this never happened again and to convert Dom to the way of the café and cake.

Chapter 23
(Visits to date 13,987 only 36,013 to go)

Despite my "Celebrity Cyclist Chrissie Wellington recommends" post being available for a few days, visitor numbers were still falling.

On the positive side, things were looking up on Twitter where I was excited to see that I had my tenth follower. It turned out that they were an online bike shop in Dublin so I wasn't really sure why they wanted to follow a cake and cycle blog based in East Anglia. My savvier social media friends, explained it was because they wanted me to follow them back. But I didn't want to play that game.

The current followers count was made up from 2 family members, 1 friend of my son, 2 cafes, 1 tourist site, a pot hole identification app, a famous cyclist I had never heard of, the fry up inspector and the online bike shop in Dublin.

I decided to write to Chrissie Wellington again to tell her about the post and cheekily ask for a retweet to her eighty thousand followers. I was worried in case she thought I was becoming a pest but she got back to me almost straight away saying she thought the post was great. As promised she tweeted a link out to her followers. This immediately shot up the post count from 19 to 168 by mid-afternoon. I immediately retweeted her tweet to my 10 followers with the good news.

Apart from the boost from the celebrity cyclist recommends post the blog was having its worst run of views. I wrote to four more cycling celebs: Emma Pooley (local Olympic cycling silver medallist), Vassos Alexandra (off Radio 2), Chris Boardman (ex-cyclist) and Micky Flanagan (a comedian who once did a TV series on cycling in France).

While I waited for their responses I decided to go back to the thing I did best and planned to blitz the blog with new posts by doing five new rides over the next seven cold and wet days. It would be a good test to see if doing lots of posting generated interest.

To kick off the week I drove up to Hard to Please House to meet up with regular cycling guest Andrew. As always, I had no idea what he had in store route and cafe wise. Normally neither does he, with the ride 'evolving organically' as we go. On arrival, and much to my surprise, Andrew proudly claimed that, not only had he a route planned (which he had marked in purple crayon on a photo copied map) but had even phoned the cafe to make sure it was open.

We had a strong wind behind so made good progress North. On the way, we discussed the latest winter cycle clothing trends as I had splashed out on new socks, gloves, base layer and florescent gilet and I was testing them all today. Unfortunately, the gilet was faulty as it had arrived with no sleeves but overall my new winter collection performed well and I was soon overheating so discarded the gloves.

We arrived at Andrew's target stop, Walsingham cafe at Great Walsingham but much to his surprise it was shut. I was also confused, as he had previously claimed to have phoned ahead. It transpired that he had only managed to speak to the answer phone which had given the opening times but failed to mention they were in an off-season closed period.

There was a message in the window explaining that the owners had gone away for a winter break but it gave a reopening date of Wednesday 15th November. Today was Thursday 13th November but I worked out the next Wednesday 15th November would be in three years so I made a note in my diary to come back then.

Not surprisingly Andrew had not got a plan B so we studied his crayoned route line on his crumpled paper map. I suggested that a short detour at the end of the route would take us to Reepham where there was a tearoom I had not tried. Andrew went into a sulk and started mumbling about having his route hijacked so we didn't exchange much banter as it was heads down into the wind for the next 15 miles to Reepham.

My plan B tearoom proved to be a big success, which made Andrew even crosser and sent him into an unprovoked rant about his dislike of Mary Berry. Despite this I recorded day one of my posting surge a success, at least from a ride perspective as again the post attracted little interest.

*****

The next day the forecast was not good, suggesting a lot of rain. However, I was determined to get these five rides in so I was pleased to find that when Big George arrived he had not seen the weather forecast showed rain all day.

The dry weather lasted less than 5 minutes before it started to drizzle. Just as we were putting on our waterproofs Big George reported that one of his brake blocks had fallen off. He said he would be fine with just a back brake. I wrestled with my conscience, in dry conditions this would probably be ok but I knew the soaking that was coming our way and felt it would be too dangerous. If Big George came off and injured himself then I would't be able to review the café. I put on my Health and Safety hat and insisted we stop at a nearby bike shop to buy replacement blocks.

The brake was quickly repaired, although by the time his bike had once again got full stopping capabilities the rain was really bucketing down. As we were still in Norwich Big George suggested we go home. I convinced him that the weather would be better the further south we went, and although I had no evidence that this was the case it seemed to make him happy.

The route I had chosen involved crossing the River Yare at Reedham on the little chain ferry. It only holds three cars and the whole crossing is over in a couple of minutes but it adds a bit of variety to a ride.

The rain continued to cascade down for the whole way until we boarded the ship (as always, I refused to pay until the ferryman had got us safely to the other side). The ferryman said we were mad to be cycling in this weather and hadn't we seen the forecast. I quickly changed the subject.

Once back on terra firma we headed south to Beccles as the rain got heavier. On entering the town, we spent some time in their mysterious one-way system. Eventually Big George used his special power of 'asking for directions' and we found our way to Twyfords Cafe.

I locked up the bikes and we went inside the café, which had a lovely European feel. There was also a big sign advertising the fact it had a secret garden. I felt having a big sign telling everyone about the garden rather took away its secret credentials but as it was still pouring with rain we decided to sit inside anyway.

Big George had cappuccino and a bacon sandwich (which is clearly not a cake). He couldn't afford a cake as he had spent most of the pocket money that Mrs Big George had allocated him on brake blocks. As we enjoyed our drinks and food the rain stopped, meaning the way back was at least dry even if we remained rather cold. I said I was planning a hot bath on my return. Big George said that it was funny, as he had just been thinking about that as well. Worried that Big George had been imagining me in the bath I quickly changed the subject to more manly things and there was no more bath chat for the rest of the way home, or ever again.

*****

After completing a third ride in three days I saw that the posts I had written were still getting a very disappointing number of views, 10 and 20 hits each. I had hoped that the more content I produced the more interest I would get but this didn't seem to be the case. It wasn't all bad news as I had seen some improvement in the number of Twitter followers, now up to 14, and the Irish online bike shop was still on board and had now been joined by a spa hotel in Hertfordshire. Word was spreading.

The final two rides of my marathon proved to be uneventful although despite the lack of excitement they attracted more post reads than more interesting ones. I still couldn't work out why different posts attracted such different numbers of readers.

By the end of November there was little to be positive about. Views on the blog had fallen right off, no new cycling celebrities had contacted me and sadly the Irish online bike shop and Hertfordshire spa hotel suddenly stopped following me.

Chapter 24
(Visits 15,138 only 34,862 to go)

I like to check my e-mail every morning, as a tidy inbox is a happy inbox. On this particular morning there was one from British Cycling saying that they would soon be having an interview with twice double gold medal track cyclist Laura Kenny and they were looking for the best questions to ask her via Twitter. As I was now part of the Twitter community it seemed like an unmissable opportunity to ask my third celebrity to give me a café to visit.

My cunning question was "Does Laura ever ride for leisure and if so which is her favourite café stop?" The interview wasn't for a couple of weeks but I was optimistic of success.

I was still many thousands of views away from my target and working out the number of hits I now required a day made things look hopeless. As most of my new ideas had failed to improve viewing figures this was my darkest hour: I needed some inspiration to get things back on track.

Before he became my cycling guest Andrew (who is notoriously hard to please) used to work with me in a boss capacity. We had spent many a happy away day, blue sky thinking and flip charting some of the finest ideas never implemented in the insurance industry. He seemed the ideal person to brainstorm some new ideas.

I invited him on a ride and after I explained the dilemma to him he claimed he had already been thinking about the problem and had several ideas to freshen up the blog. As he went through his list it was clear that most of them centred around writing less about cake and more about things he was interested in. Although I wouldn't be including any obscure Italian poetry in future he did point out that maybe the balance of the blog had started to be a bit too cake-centric. To attempt to redress the balance I came up with a new feature called Cycling Guest's Cycling Top Tip.

This was the first tip from Andrew.

Cycling guests cycling top tip No 1. For a smoother and more efficient ride, make sure your tyres are pumped up to the correct pressure.

It was quite a dull tip but it got the ball rolling and I was sure future guests would come up with better ones (they didn't).

With Andrew continuing to share his blog improvement ideas the ride down to Bungay went smoothly and we soon arrived at Jesters of Bungay. It turned out that not only is Jesters of Bungay a cafe in Bungay but also doubles up as the visitor's centre for Bungay castle.

On arrival, we found a large outdoor seating area which also provided information on Bungay castle via a multimedia model castle display exhibit (MMCDE). I studied the MMCDE and discovered that Bungay Castle was built in the 1100's by a chap called Hugh Bigod who used Bungay as his power base when trying to overthrow the King. He failed but if he had won Bungay could now be the Capital of England.

Whilst waiting for our cakes and drinks to arrive Andrew, once again, revealed more of his anti-cake views. On our last trip, he had shockingly revealed he was not a fan of cake queen Mary Berry and today followed this up with the suggestion that there should be fewer cake photos in my blog as when you have seen one piece of cake etc. I decided to ignore his worrying cake-ist views.

Instead I brought him up to date with "Celebrity cyclist recommends" news. After the early wins of Chrissey Wellington and Boris Johnson I hadn't heard back from any of the other cycling celebrities. I would have to spread my net further to include any celebrity even if they didn't cycle. He checked his address book but confirmed he didn't know any celebrities either.

Back at Crusader Towers I flicked through Twitter and came across a tweet from British Cycling with the date of the Laura Kenny interview. I realised I wouldn't know if Laura had answered my tweeted question, let alone whether she had given me a café recommendation, until next week. Well I could forget about trying to get any sleep for the next few days with that level of suspense hanging over me. No point even going to bed.

During all this on-line activity, I noticed that the next day was the hideous American import of Black Friday. However, I noticed that the term Black Friday was the most searched term on the internet which gave me a cunning idea.

With rain forecast and dark skies I quickly arranged a ride and called the post 'Black Friday' in a cynical attempt to use the current most popular search engine term to get more blog hits.

Despite getting him soaked on our last ride, Big George agreed to be my guest for the 50 mile loop up to Itteringham, a small village in Norfolk. On the way, I told him about my new feature; cycling guest's cycling top tip. He was very excited and after much consideration came up with his tip.

Cycling guests cycling top tip No 2. To avoid punctures and skidding on your winter rides it is worth fitting some heavy duty 700c-25 winter tyres on your road bike.

I didn't like to point out that despite following cycling guest cycling top tip No 2 at the start of the winter I had had a puncture on yesterday's ride but I thought I wouldn't undermine his effort.

Once we had crossed Norwich the ride out to Itteringham was very pleasant, if a bit dark, and we arrived successfully at Itteringham cafe and community shop. I have noticed many of this type of village stores cropping up. They are owned and run by the local community where residents volunteer to run the shop on a rota basis. This often leads to an inconsistent customer experience especially if the person in front of you is a friend of today's staff member and needs to bring them up to date with their personal trivia.

It was easily the smallest cafe I had so far found on my quest as it had only two tables in the corner of the shop and a couple of benches outside but thanks to its community status it had a lovely cosy country folk atmosphere and so got a high Atmosphere and Ambiance (AAA) score.

As well as the mandatory cake, we also decided to have sausage rolls. There was a choice of two, on which today's community volunteer turned out to be an expert. After a long and informative talk about each roll I decided to try the one made from rare breed pork. I was immediately filled with guilt when I realised the few remaining rare pigs were being turned into sausage rolls. After the first bite, however, it became clear that it was one of the best sausage rolls I had ever had and well worth putting a few pigs' long-term future at risk.

Overall the Itteringham Shop and Cafe had been a very good stop and was a bit different from your run of the mill cafe. As you can imagine with a local community shop it is the hub for local inhabitants so while we were there much local village drama was played out. It was a bit like listening to the Archers (which I don't) in real time. I can't tell you what I heard because what happens in Itteringham stays in Itteringham.

After posting I was disappointed to see my plan had failed as once again the post count struggled. I thought more about my cunning idea and realised that the term Black Friday would bring up an awful lot of hits so I was unlikely to end up on the first few hundred pages on such an internet search. I filed the idea in my rubbish plans drawer which was now getting rather full.

Finally it was time for the Laura Kenny Q&A session to be broadcast. British cycling had asked them in the form of a video so I excitedly clicked on the link and waited for my question to be answered. The video was 3 minutes long and had a rather predictable stream of questions.

Q. What training should you do to become a good sprinter.

Laura. I don't know as I'm naturally good at sprinting, I just do lots of fast cycling.

Q. What turbo training do you recommend.

Laura. I don't know as I don't use one and just do lots of fast cycling.

Q. What road races are you doing next year.

Laura. I don't know yet but I'll be cycling them fast

After a couple of minutes, it was clear we were not finding out very much about Laura. What the public really wanted to know was what was her favourite café cycle venue although judging by the rest of her answers it looked likely that she wouldn't have known anyway. Disappointedly I decided I would have to park Laura and chase some different celebrities.

Chapter 25
(Visits 15,765 only 34,235 to go)

By the start of December, I still needed to average 120 people a day wanting to know where to cycle for a half decent bit of cake in the Norfolk area. On one hand, it seemed a doable task as I had had occasional days hitting the 120 mark, but on the other, were there really 120 people in Norfolk planning a cake-based cycle ride every day? I put such negative thoughts to the back of my mind and decided to crack on with another ride that featured history.

As always, Big George was late for the start and 15 minutes had passed before I got the excuse text. This time he would be late as he had a puncture, apparently. I thought this a little ironic, or possibly a lie, as the cycling guest cycling top tip he had offered on our last ride was to put on thick winter tyres to avoid such things, which he had done. If it really was a puncture it completely undermine my new cycling guest cycling top tip feature. If I got another useless top tip today I might have to scrap the whole idea or risk litigation, I just hoped it would be a good one.

When he eventually arrived, I explained we were going to ride out to Lincoln's Tea and Coffee Shoppe in Hingham. After the success of my informative recent history-based post to Bungay Castle I decided history buffs wanted more facts so I had done some pre-ride research. Apparently, Abraham Lincoln, the famous American President, had ancestors who emigrated from Hingham to America in 1637. It makes you think: if they hadn't emigrated Abraham Lincoln would probably have become our British Prime Minister and Hingham our capital city. There is no evidence that Abraham Lincoln ever visited the Tea and Coffee Shoppe named after his family, so it was left to me to check it out on his behalf.

On the way, I asked Big George for his useless cycling tip suggestion for the new feature and fortunately he didn't disappoint with an absolute corker.

Guest cyclist top cycling tip No 4. To make yourself visible when signalling to other road users, wear fluorescent yellow or orange cycling mitts.

Pure genius, although it transpired that Big George only purchased his Hi-Viz mitts as they were on special offer and not for health and safety reasons. I was also surprised he wasn't wearing them today. He explained that they are only suitable for warm weather summer rides (when visibility is good anyway).

Lincoln's have cleverly called themselves a Tea and Coffee *Shoppe* to give it an olde worlde feel from the days when lots of words had an extra e on the end. This is just the sort of thing Big George hates and once he saw the dining area had table-cloths and lace curtains he refused to go in. I eventually persuaded him to sit in the comfy chairs provided in the reception area by the door.

While on the ride I had some good news. The latest edition of the Norwich Cycling Campaign newsletter had been published and I was excited to see the café-based article I had sent them had made a full page, occupying a tenth of the total newsletter content. It was my first published article so I felt I could now consider myself a proper writer and immediately added the fact to my CV.

By the end of the next day there had been no visitor spike which meant either the distribution of the newsletter is very small or no one reads it or more likely both.

*****

As Christmas approached I completed several more rides while my Twitter followers grew to an impressive 26 but despite this blog traffic continued to fall, some days not even getting to 20.

The trouble with this time of year for the cafe cycle reviewer is that everyone's thoughts begin to turn to Christmas. Fewer cafes are open nor cycle guests available, so I was glad when Mrs Crusader and Barry and Helen and their tandem volunteered for a ride.

Barry had recently upgraded his cycling GPS so I had put him in charge of today's route which started from Sainsbury's car park near his house. It wasn't far into the route when we reached a nice long stretch of cycle path by the side of a completely empty road. Shockingly Barry and Helen and their tandem refused to use it as they had not been directed to by Barry's new cycling GPS. Mrs Crusader, as a former member of the Tufty the Squirrel road safety club (and she used to have a badge to prove it), was appalled. Whenever there is a potentially dangerous road traffic situation she always asks herself what would Tufty the Squirrel have done and, clearly, he would have made me join her safely on the cycle path, so I did. With Barry and Helen and their tandem acting like Willy Weasel and laughing in the face of Tufty they were lucky that they made it to the café at all.

Once there, I told my guests that British Cycling seemed to have copied my cycling tip feature as they had put a top 10 winter tips article on their website and had advertised it on Twitter. I was shocked when I got to their winter tip 4. It said:"ditch the cafe stop."

Their rationale was that you are likely to keep your coat on in the cafe and not feel the benefit when you go outside again. This is the level of advice I expect from my mother and not a well-respected organisation like British Cycling so I suggest you ignore their top winter tips and stick to the ones provided by my knowledgeable cycling guests.

Unfortunately, neither Mrs Crusader, Barry or Helen could come up with a decent tip on this ride so it was left to Barry and Helen's Tandem to give me a worthwhile suggestion.

Cycling Guest top cycling tip No 7. Don't cycle unnecessarily through puddles as your bike gets cold, wet, muddy and very unhappy.

*****

The highlight from my pre-Christmas rides was getting two new loyalty cards to add to my loyalty card picture library, but even after sharing this news there was not a rush of people to view it. I decided I needed a new distribution stream so set up a dedicated Cake Crusader Facebook page.

And there was some good news: Poppy's café (the best café or tearoom between London and Paris that I happened to stop at) claimed to be very excited about the certificate that I had sent them, which they had now put on display. However, there was still no news from the Hotel Vitranc (European Café of the year), which meant the following year I found myself there again attempting to present it in person.

My recent ideas had all failed to generate new interest but while reading the reviews of the year I came up with something that did generate some blog interest and things started to look up.

Chapter 26
(Visits 16,300 only 33,700 to go)

I had noticed it was awards season so I tweeted that I would announce a Cake Crusader Cycle Café category winner every day on Twitter during Christmas week. I was sure my 30 followers would be excited by the news. There would be a winner in each of my five reviewing categories plus the overall café or tearoom of the year.

As preparation for the big award I needed to revisit Earsham street café. Ever since my first visit it had been my number one rated cafe. However, I had not returned in over a year and having now reviewed over seventy cafes and tea rooms, I was keen to make sure that standards had been maintained.

As this was such an important ride I had asked Andrew to be my guest today to really put them through their paces and he didn't disappoint. As Earsham Street Cafe always seems to be busy we left a bit earlier to avoid the lunch-time rush. This turned out to be a huge mistake.

The ride down was uneventful and we arrived, as planned, at 11:30.

One of the best features at Earsham Street Cafe is that they let you wheel your bikes through to the outdoor seating area at the back. Although the outdoor seating area is very sheltered, being December, we decided to sit in the main indoor seating area. We found a table where I got out my phone and located the cafe ratings spreadsheet ready for today's critical update. The first category was effective cake selection (ECS) so we went to check out the cakes, which were on display in the window. Although not the biggest selection there was plenty to choose from and they all looked very tempting. This made the cake selection very effective and got it a high ECS score consistent with previous visits.

We moved on to ordering and I went for hot chocolate, chocolate and orange cake plus a cheese scone so that I could do an in-depth cake taste quality (CTQ) test. Andrew ordered a cappuccino, lemon drizzle cake and decided he wanted a hummus sandwich as well. It was at this point that things started to unwind as the nice waitress pointed out that Andrew couldn't have a hummus sandwich as it was part of the lunchtime menu which didn't come into operation until 12 o'clock which was still 25 minutes away.

She explained chef was busy preparing for lunch to make sure everything was ready and fresh. Instead, Andrew could have a bacon sandwich as this was on the breakfast menu, which was still available. As a faddy vegetarian, this wasn't an acceptable solution so he declined the offer and just went with cake.

Obviously, such an incident sent Andrew off into a rant but as we are British his rant got directed at me rather than the Earsham Street Cafe staff. His main point seemed a good one; cooking bacon and making it into a sandwich was likely to distract chef from his lunchtime preparation far more than slapping a bit of hummus on to some bread. I had to agree with him but moaning to me about it wasn't really going to help fulfil his sandwich needs.

After some time, not helped by other customers ordering bacon sandwiches, I managed to calm him down and get him refocused on the matter in hand. I was worried the hummus sandwich incident (HSI) would affect his rating judgement but as sandwiches form no part of my cycle cafe scoring system it was important that this matter was parked for now. Andrew may be notoriously hard to please but showed great professionalism as we returned to discuss the atmosphere and ambiance rating.

Our drinks and cakes arrived and all looked very good. The only disappointment was that my cheese scone hadn't been warmed up in the way a cheese scone should be. I didn't like to ask if it could be in case it distracted chef further from any pressing lunchtime matters.

The hot chocolate was excellent, nice and thick, a good temperature and very chocolatey. Andrew thought his cappuccino was very good although it could have been slightly stronger for absolute top marks.

I entered all the ratings, into the spreadsheet and Earsham Street Cafe was still at the top with just the CTQ score to come. It wasn't in the bag yet as they would still need a very high CTQ rating to hold on to top spot. With some trepidation, we tucked into our cakes. I knew what I thought straight away but from his face I couldn't tell which way Andrew was going to go with his lemon drizzle. I asked his opinion and after the correctly timed dramatic pause he announced that it was a fab-u-lous piece of cake. I also thought the chocolate and orange cake I had was one of the best cakes of this year and despite it not being warm the cheese scone was top drawer too. The high CTQ score was entered and the final scores were in.

Despite the HSI and the cold cheese scone the Earsham Street Cafe had improved its average rating by 0.03 to extend its lead as the Cake Crusader number 1 rated cafe. Andrew, who was obviously feeling guilty about his rant, even left a tip, which is unheard of, as we both agreed it deserved its place at the top of the leader board.

I was just leaving the café when an old chap approached me and clearly wanted to engage in conversation. He asked me the unexpected question of 'do I ring my bell when overtaking dog walkers?' I had to admit I didn't. If he had looked at my bike he would have seen that I didn't have a bell although I couldn't help but notice nor did he have a dog.

He said I needed to ring my bell as when cyclists ride up behind dog walkers going at 30 mph (I assume the cyclist not the dog walker) the dogs can't hear you coming and get spooked. I said that I only wished that I could cycle at 30 mph and was even less likely to be able to by adding the weight of a bell to my bike. However, I promised to take his advice on board and that I would pass on his request to other cyclists. True to my word when I got home I included in my post of the ride a special one-off feature.

Complete stranger coming up to you in the street top cycling tip no 1. When going at 30mph on your bike make sure you ring your bell when overtaking dog walkers so as not to spook the dog.

*****

With everything now in place, it was time to launch the 1st Cake Crusader Annual café and tearoom awards. I went through my records and found the highest marks awarded in each category. I then tweeted out the winner along with the original post. When deciding on the winners I had applied a "no café e-mail address no prize" rule in order that I could email one of my coveted homemade winner's certificate to the chosen café so they had something to commemorate their achievement. I assumed most of the winners would not bother to print the certificates and proudly display them but you have to try.

This was the first time one of my ideas had worked, as the cafes were all very excited when I gave them the news and sent them their certificates. The bonus was that the original post saw their counts nudge up a bit too.

At the start of the year it hit me that there was something else missing in my approach. When I used to have better things to do with my time, I had something called a job. I remembered that at the start of each year great importance was put on setting and reviewing objectives and goals.

After several minutes' thought I had put several excellent objectives in place which, combined with a new data capture spreadsheet on my phone, would allow me to produce a quarterly progress report and give myself everything I needed for a full end of year cycle café performance review.

The cycle cafe goals (and measures) I came up with were:

1. **Cycle to more than the 80 different cafes I visited last year by avoiding any more near death experiences over the next 12 months.** *(Measure: number of cafes visited greater than 80, number near death experiences less than 1)*
2. **Campaign to stop cafes serving cake on top of the serviette as this renders them useless for mouth wiping activity** *(Measure: Cake serviette serving coefficient is greater than 80%)*
3. **Encourage all cafes to follow the old rhyme 'cheese Scone hot, fruit scone not' at all times** *(Measure: Cheese scones served warm over 90%)*
4. **Record the data required to produce a quarterly progress report and even more fascinating cycle/cafe/cake related facts.** *(Measure: Produce Quarterly report of cafe/cycle/cake facts and publish end of year performance review write up)*
5. **Break the world record for most cafes visited on a calorie neutral bike ride in one day** *(Measure: Cycle to 20 cafes in one day as per the official calorie neutral bike ride rules)*

Once I had put these bad boys in place I felt much happier knowing I was now operating with the sort of governance any self-respecting cycle café reviewer should have in place. Just as in the real world, I never looked at them again.

*****

With all the foundations in place, and after an extended Cafe Cycle Christmas break it was good to get back on the bike. As storms and winds were coming our way I had decided it would be best to take it easy for the first ride and train into the wind before cycling back with the wind. I met up with cycle guest, Big George, at Norwich station to catch the train down to Thetford. I had a route planned via Watton where we planned to find a café. It would also be the first chance to test out my beta version of the new improved data capture spreadsheet on my phone.

The ride got off to a bad start when Big George told me that Mrs Big George had not given him permission to go out riding today and instead had given him a to do list. The two key dos on the list were to take down the outside Christmas lights and buy toilet paper. I said that it didn't sound a particularly challenging to do list and he should to be able to fit it in after we got back. However Big George said that to do the lights he had to go up on the roof (the Drifters weren't available) which required daylight as, although he wasn't scared of heights or the dark individually, he was if they were combined. We worked out that if we got back by 2:30 he would have time to get up on the roof in the light and still get to the shops for the toilet paper. It would mean going fast and cutting down our cafe stopping time but should be possible and Mrs Big George would be none the wiser.

Whilst on the train I decided the saddle on the new bike Santa had brought me needed raising and so I took my saddle tool bag off to retrieve the appropriate seat adjustment tool. On leaving the train at Thetford I realised the saddle bag was still on the train, which was no longer in the station. There was nothing I could do but go back to the ticket office and reported the missing bag to a very helpful ticket lady.

We were now well behind schedule and the wind and rain might not be the only storm Big George would face today. I also now had no spare inner tubes, tyre levers, or bike tools but fortunately I hadn't had a puncture for ages so what were the chances of getting one today.

As it turned out very high. After just a few miles my front tyre went flat. We had no inner tubes the right size but Big George had one remaining puncture patch in his tool bag. Using the law of market forces, that I had taught him in France, he was prepared to sell it to me at a vastly inflated rate. I was left with no choice but to meet his outrageous demands and using the world's most expensive patch I successfully repaired the leak. After a short while, we were off again but the chance of Big George getting up on the roof today was now looking slim.

We arrived in Watton we found Adem's Cafe on the High Street. It was more at the greasy spoon rather than Victorian tearoom end of the cafe continuum but Big George much prefers that end anyway so he was happy.

I had given each of my goals for the year a column on my new improved cycle cafe spreadsheet. I was looking forward to seeing what Adem's cafe serviette policy was and was pleased to see it was delivered separately to the cake so full marks there and an 'off' in the napkin/cake serving status spreadsheet cell.

Despite cutting our coffee and cake chat to a minimum, when we left we were a long way behind the clock. In our favour, the weather was building up behind us and the wind gave us the extra speed we needed. Fearing the wrath of Mrs Big George, we went flat out and thankfully got home just in time. Big George went straight back to get his ladder out and I went home to follow step one of the Abellio train lost property process. Despite several attempts my bag was never found.

With more rides completed through January and the Cake Crusader Award winners all announced I had taken my eye off the ball nearer to home when I discovered that I had missed my 25th (silver) wedding anniversary by a day. I didn't consider it my fault as no one had told me until it was too late so the day had passed card and gift free, which I'm told is bad. What better way to make it up, I thought, than to invite Mrs Crusader to be my cycling guest on a freezing cold cafe cycle review where I would be buying the cake! I certainly know how to win a lady round.

As it was -2 C I decided on a short ride down to the recently opened Garden Tea Rooms in Wymondham. On the way, I asked Mrs Crusader for her cycling guest top cycling tip.

Cycling guests cycling top tip no 11. To avoid an even frostier cafe cycle ride, try to remember the date of your 25th wedding anniversary and act on it accordingly.

It was cold in all senses of the word as we arrived at the Garden Tea Rooms. My Alarmio lock had recently died so I had purchased a new super strong lock to deter any potential bike crime. I spent some time attempting to lock our bikes using what can only be described as the Rubik cube of bike security, before eventually solving the puzzle and going inside.

The Garden Tea Rooms were nice and light and the owner was also very cycle friendly. She explained that on request, cyclists can take their bikes round the back to the outdoor seating area rather than needing to lock them out on the street.

Next, I tried to take a photo of the cake selection but was blocked by a lady who wanted coffee and cake. She insisted on the ingredients of each cake being listed before deciding it had eggs in it. When all the cakes had been gone through she explained she was allergic to eggs. Again, information that would have been useful much earlier on in the process. In the end, she went for soup, which, being a bit of an expert on the subject, is not cake and a glass of water, which is not coffee. I immediately decided not to invite her to become a cycling guest as she would be a useless reviewer and probably didn't have a bike anyway.

There was a small but effective collection featuring a Devils chocolate cake as the star offering. With my Hot Chocolate, I obviously ordered the Devils chocolate cake. As it is a rule that we can't both have the same cake I got Mrs Crusader a brown fruit scone as it looked like a healthy option. As it was our anniversary I kindly let her have a very small bit of my chocolate cake as well (you can see why I'm a keeper).

We set off for home in the arctic conditions and were soon frozen once again. Although the ride had gone well I'm not entirely sure it had made up for my anniversary faux pas so I plan to try harder for our Golden Anniversary in twenty-five years' time and maybe even let her choose her own cake that day.

I was pleased with the start of the year. Some good rides completed, some success with café award and objectives for the year were in place. I now just had to become an internet sensation. This was certainly not the time to rest on my laurels.

Chapter 27
(Visits 18,500 only 31,500 to go)

The main problem with riding in February is the unpredictable weather, especially as most of my cycling guests were wimps. Playing the 'but you're a hard man, beer drinking rugby fan' card, I persuaded Big George to come out on a very cold February day.

When he turned up for the start he was still worried about conditions but I said that he would be fine (as it turned out he wasn't). The main topic of conversation turned to future trip planning as I needed a guest to take on my next "celebrity cyclist recommends" ride scheduled for a few weeks' time. To encourage him to come along I let him into the secret of who the celebrity was and where we were going. He got very excited about the prospect and this giddy mindset may well have been a factor in what happened next as we almost had a major cycling incident (MCI).

Up until this point the roads had all been fine and my decision to go ahead with the ride had appeared to be a good one. Then we came across a very shady stretch of road where we hit a large patch of ice. Big George lost control and slid off his bike right in front of me. I was unable to halt in time, and instead of being able to use my normal braking system I had to resort to riding into Big George's back as a makeshift stopping device. This sent me flying over the handle bars but luckily I landed on the soft verge. There were bikes, bottles, pumps and people splattered across the road and a car could easily have come along at any moment putting us into serious peril and causing an actual MCI.

Thanks to my quick-thinking I was able to get my phone out and take a photo of the carnage before any clearing up had started. It was a huge relief as I now had a photo of the MCI to post.

With the photo safely captured, and despite it being his fault, I kindly checked to see if Big George was alright. He was a bit shaken and had hurt his hip and back but he was fit enough to continue to the cafe (which was all I really cared about).

We tentatively continued our journey and eventually crawled into Attleborough where we found Bailey's cafe on the high street overlooking the green. There was limited outdoor seating but at this temperature we were likely to get frozen to the metal chairs so we went inside.

I ordered cake, mandatory cheese scone and a hot chocolate. Big George was clearly still suffering from shock as he ordered crumpets and Marmite. Not only is crumpet and Marmite not cake but I didn't even know it was a thing. In his current mental state, I felt it would be dangerous for Big George to take part in any further cafe rating today so I finished the scoring on my own.

Bailey's cafe turned out to be a very cheap one. As Big George clearly didn't know what time of day it was I didn't tell him that he had paid for both of us when he thought he was just paying his share of the bill.

Bashed and bruised we took it easy on the way back. Big George did mention that he was surprised how expensive crumpet and Marmite was but I told him that's because it wasn't really a thing and he seemed happy.

*****

To keep up momentum I was now on the lookout for new demographic groups to attract to the site, and it was at this point that I was presented with such an opportunity.

Andrew had recently become interested in birds (the feathered variety), which he claimed was because he is old and all old people become interested in birds. I'm hoping to be old one day so I thought it was about time I found out more on the subject. The easiest approach was to take a ride to Cley Marshes visitors' centre where I could see birds and rate a cafe.

It was another cold and damp day but we pedalled hard giving us time for plenty of bird action.

The centre is a very modern building, which has a huge windowed indoor seating area overlooking the marshes. This area was full of actual bird watchers taking part in today's competition. There were also a few tables for fans to watch the competitors and it was there we opted to sit.

Before we tried the cakes and drinks Andrew taught me a few bird spotting basics. Flying seemed to be key and I felt that I quickly got the hang of it although there didn't seem to be a set of proper rules. As my confidence grew I really got into it and as things flew past the window I was able to identify them as actual birds. To create a bit more atmosphere I took to pointing and shouting "bird" making sure all my fellow twitchers didn't miss out on the one I had spotted.

Just then a particularly good bird flew past, which I assumed scored you extra points. I knew it must have been a good one because some of the players in the prime bird watching seats stood up. I was very pleased to have seen such a good bird although I had no idea what it was.

When the excitement had died down I went back to cake tasting and completed the café review.

At the end of our visit I asked at the information desk what was the winning score for the day. I was told it didn't work like that. Apparently, bird watching isn't a sport it's just a thing. I didn't understand this concept and decided I couldn't take part in an activity that didn't have a winner, scoring system or league tables.

On our way home Andrew said he was glad we had ignored the poor weather forecast and had come out on the ride. After such a foolish remark, there was only one thing that could possibly happen and within a few minutes we were being bombarded with stinging hail followed by sleet and snow. Andrew may be old and know about birds but he still has a lot to learn about commenting on weather conditions while out on a cycle ride.

I hoped the post would attract the yet to be exploited bird watching community to the blog. I was therefore very pleased to see that views quickly got up to 100. This still may not be internet sensation standard but was a great improvement from the early days when it was several months before my first post hit that mark. In fact, all my recent posts were now hovering around this figure so I was pleased with progress.

With confidence growing I decided to invite Barry (and Helen and their Tandem) to be cycling guests so I could let Barry know that interest in the blog was growing.

Although they don't look it, Barry and Helen must also be old as they had just returned from a bird watching holiday in Mexico. I was excited to tell them that I too had recently been bird watching as well. I told them they could read about it on the blog. Helen said she was already up to date with the posts but Barry took yet another opportunity to remind me that he couldn't see the point of my blog or indeed any blog (except for the one by the Fry Up Inspector as knowing where he could get a good fried breakfast was useful to him) so he had no intention of reading about it.

After a period of silent cycling I spotted a large sign, in the shape of a teapot, pointing to the Olive Branch, which was today's destination. I was a little surprised to see it at this point in the ride as I knew it was still some way to go so I decided to measure how far the sign was from the tea room.

It was 4.3 miles later that we arrived at the Olive Branch which I noted down on my café cycle data capture spreadsheet cycling records tab as a new sign to cafe differential record. History told me that the Guinness book of so called world records wouldn't be interested even if I could have been bothered to tell them (which I did and they weren't).

After we had settled into the Olive branch indoor seating area the cakes, scones and drinks arrived but to my horror the cake was on top of the serviette. I took a photo and added it to my #keepcakesoffserviettes on Twitter.

I asked Barry, Helen and their tandem if they had a cycling guest cycling top tip for me today. I was surprised when Barry said he did.

Cycling Guest Cycling top tip No. 14. When out on a cycle ride don't waste yours and everyone else's time by photographing everything you see (especially cake) for a pointless blog, unless the blog is about fried breakfast.

*****

After a deafening silence from most of the celebrity cyclists I had contacted, I thought I would try writing to my local MPs. It was a good scam as I knew they always responded to their constituent's requests.

I started with my local Norwich MPs and went straight to Wikipedia. It said that North Norwich MP Chloe Smith is a keen cyclist so, despite there being a disappointing lack of cake references on her page, Chloe seemed an ideal political cycling celebrity candidate.

A few days after writing I was excited to see that Chloe had replied to my e-mail with some cafe and route suggestions. As you know Wikipedia is not always the most reliable source so I was worried in case the cycling bit had been made up but Chloe confirmed she does love to get out on the bike and uses a hybrid or road bike in Norfolk. So, another 'cycling celebrity' ride was in the bag.

Meanwhile, my planning for the Boris Johnson ride was going well but before I could enter the world of political cycling celebrities I needed to check that Big George was recovered, both physically and mentally, after his recent fall and still up for the Boris trip.

On the day of his fitness test I noted that strong winds from the south were forecast. So as not to make the ride too hard I repeated my favourite trick of taking the train to Lowestoft and going to Southwold from there before returning to Norwich with the wind behind.

One important thing to do when planning a ride is to make sure your cafe cycle stop comes at least halfway through, and preferably nearer the end than the beginning of the route. This is to make sure you don't run out of steam as you enter the final few miles. Due to the use of the train our planned stop would be less than a quarter of the way into the journey, rule book meet the waste paper bin. Combining this with doing the ride on Friday 13th just showed how mad and crazy I could be but that's just my carefree unregulated approach to life. I was, however, slightly annoyed with Big George's faffing about at Lowestoft station causing us to set off nearly three minutes behind schedule.

With the wind into our faces for the first few miles down to Southwold it was still hard work and we were quite puffed out when we arrived at Fifty-One Southwold.

There were no cheese scones available so I had a sausage roll. Big George was very pleased with the lack of cheese scones as he is always tempted by until he remembers he doesn't actually like them. He was much happier with the sausage roll option.

Although not cake and therefore not part of my cafe rating system, the sausage rolls were very good, so good, in fact, that Big George kept going on about how nice his sausage roll was all the way home (which I hoped wasn't a euphemism).

We now had a long ride back to Norwich albeit with the wind behind but my carefree craziness proved costly as Big George ran out of puff with a few miles to go and we had to crawl along for the last part. When I got home I had to retrieve the rule book from the bin. I would not make the same mistake for Boris's ride.

Chapter 28
(Visits 19,945 only 30,065 to go)

There were only seven months to go in which to become an internet sensation. I had been at it for nearly 18 months and noticed I was about to do my 100th Café visit so the next ride would be a special one.

I had chosen Andrew to be my 100th cafe review cycling guest as he was also my first. This was a risk as you may remember that he had proved to be a very poor guest on my special 1st anniversary cafe cycle ride a few months ago, when he had failed to provide a card, balloons or candles at any point during the trip. It appeared that nothing had changed as he again turned out to be an equally useless and grumpy 100th cafe review cycling guest.

I was now in the habit of always checking the weather forecast before a ride and it did not look good for this one. It showed a lot of heavy rain was due. I was therefore not surprised to receive a text from Andrew saying that he would rather stay dry than go out today. As it was a special one I really wanted to do it so decided that the best approach was to ignore the text and just turn up on his door step at the allotted meeting time, which I did. You can't call yourself the Cake Crusader and not go on a planned ride because of a few spots of rain. On arrival, I pointed out what a momentous ride this was and that if he had read the BBC forecast in detail, and not just looked at the pictures, he would have known that it actually said there would be some showers between dry spells which didn't sound too bad. Added to this, today's venue was the Art Cafe at Glandford which, like Andrew, is vegetarian. He therefore reluctantly agreed to come along and as a compromise I said we could go the direct route rather than the pretty way.

The weather forecast proved to be 50% correct as it got the rain part right but the bit about dry spells in between was inaccurate. This wasn't altogether surprising as I had made that bit up to encourage

Andrew to come along. In these conditions, we soon found ourselves extremely wet.

Things went from bad to worse when Andrew got a puncture. In these circumstances, it was a difficult job and by the time he had finished fixing it he could no longer feel his fingers. It was the final nail in the cheerful banter coffin as we rode in silence for the rest of the way out to the cafe.

As we approached Glandford things started to look up as I pointed out that the cows in the adjacent field were now standing up and we all know this means it was shortly going to stop raining. Andrew didn't seem convinced as he doesn't trust, or eat, cows.

With another one of those weird coincidences the Art Cafe is next door to an actual art gallery! It has a nice outdoor seating area but despite the positive sign from the cows Andrew was keen that we went inside. This was a good plan as we were quickly directed to a table by the log burner to dry off.

We ordered cakes and a mandatory cheese scone. I ordered my hot chocolate and was given a choice of sweetness, a first. I like a stronger bitter drink so plumped for the dark hot chocolate. Andrew was given a choice of four different coffee beans to choose from plus a choice of ways it could be brewed. This was the Art Cafe's only mistake of the day as Andrew is not only notoriously hard to please and a very poor special ride guest but does not respond well to being given choices. It sent him into options meltdown and he was unable to function. I had to step in and randomly order Nicaragua beans aero pressed or we would still be there now.

While we waited for the cakes and drinks I asked Andrew if he had brought me a card, balloons or candles to mark the 100th cafe review occasion. He had not but he did then surprise me by going to the counter to splash out 60p on the Art Café cheese scone recipe card. I suppose it is the thought that counts.

Our cakes and drinks were excellent, meaning the Art Café was rated as one of my top cafes. The fire had dried off our wet things and now, full of cake and warmed by our drinks, we were in a much better mood as we headed for the door to remount our bikes.

Once outside we discovered that the local cows clearly didn't know what they were mooing about as it was still pouring with rain. I popped my helmet back on and got a nasty soaking from the soggy head comfort sponges inside. On the return to Aylsham we continued to get wetter, although there was still time to round the ride off nicely with one last puncture.

It eventually stopped raining just as we arrived back at HTPH where Andrew gave me his cycling guest cycling top tip.

Cycling guest cycling top tip no. 17. If you want to avoid getting soaking wet and freezing cold on a bike ride then don't ignore the weather forecast when it includes words like heavy, persistent, down pour and rain.

*****

There was another anniversary to celebrate as it had been a year since my NDE so I had planned 13 rides (take that Dr Superstition) during the month of March. The highlight would be the Boris Johnson celebrity cyclist recommends ride. As I now had improving visitor figures and a number of special events and rides planned I wanted to bring Barry up to speed and make him sweat.

As usual he quickly crushed my enthusiasm by pointing out I still need over 30,000 visits in the next seven months and as I had only managed 20,000 up to now he felt his bet was still safe.

There was a good start to my March cycling madness but I was pinning my hopes on the Boris ride. I had written to Former Mayor of London Boris Johnson for his top cafe and cycle route recommendation some time ago and I had been very excited when I got the following reply.

Dear Kevin,

Thank you for your email. Boris has asked Andrew Gilligan his former London Cycling Commissioner to get back to you about this. Andrew's favourite café is the Buenos Aires Café.

I do hope this helps with your blog and I wish you the best of luck for the future,

Yours sincerely,

Nick
Transport Team, Greater London Authority

It was clear that Boris obviously liked my blog as he had personally asked his former cycling commissioner from his mayoral days, for input.

On further inspection, I thought that the Buenos Aires cafe seemed a strange choice as Brazil seemed a long way away to go for a cycle ride. After a little on-line research, it turned out the cafe was in Greenwich which was a much more manageable proposition. As no route had been suggested I sent off for some free Transport for London (TFL) cycle maps and planned a nice 60-mile round trip route starting at Tilbury docks in Kent, going to Greenwich and returning on the official Thames cycle path. It had taken me five months from first getting his reply to have everything in place so I was confident nothing would go wrong.

I had decided to drive down to the start, so Big George and I set off down to Kent to see if we could find the Buenos Aires cafe while also taking the opportunity to check out the capital's cycling infrastructure.

After a two-hour drive we arrived at Tilbury and found somewhere to park. There followed traditional pre-ride faffing before we were ready to set off.

First, we had to negotiate crossing the M25, which is a motorway. We don't have motorways in Norfolk so this was a new experience and involved many roundabouts and bridges but we made it to the other side in one piece. Then we got lost at the Lakeside out of town shopping centre. We don't have out of town shopping centres in Norfolk but apparently you are not meant to cycle inside them.

After one final diversion, past an accident, we eventually made it to cycling super highway 3 (CS3) which would take us most of the rest of the way.

The only way you knew it was a cycling super highway was that it had blue tarmac. We only saw one other cyclist on a 5 mile stretch. It was a bit disappointing that for a city of 10 million only 1 person appeared to use it.

Thanks to the cycling super highway we quickly made it to the wrong side of the Thames. The TFL map said this was where we should cross but I couldn't see any sign of a bridge. After some wandering around I discovered that there was a passenger tunnel under the Thames. It had strict no cycling signs which we obeyed by correctly walking our bikes under the river before climbing the stairs and finding ourselves by the Cutty Sark, just around the corner from the Buenos Aires cafe in Greenwich.

Outside was a continental style outdoor pavement seating area. I locked our bikes while Big George went inside to find us some seats. It was now time to implement the next part of my plan as from under my cycle top I produced a cardboard Boris Johnson mask. Big George took one look at it and guessed what I had in mind. Being a proud Scotsman, he was not keen to take part and play the role of Boris so that I could take some fake publicity photos. I promised to buy him his lunch so being a proud Scotsman he agreed.

There was a very good variety of lovely looking cakes available so I awarded a high effective cake selection (ECS) rating and chose the chocolate and nut. Boris went for orange and chocolate cake with a filter coffee.

Inside the cafe had a selection of wooden chair and leather sofa seating areas. The walls were decorated with random Argentinian memorabilia to make it feel more like Buenos Aires (it didn't).

Our food and drinks turned up and we could get down to rating. I'm sure Boris would be pleased to hear that Andrew Gilligan (his former cycling commissioner) had come up trumps with his recommendation.

The route back was going to be on the official Thames cycle path, along the South bank, which would take us all the way to the Ferry port at Gravesend. I had downloaded the route from the official site and loaded it on to my bike sat nav. However first we had to get from the cafe to the start of the return route. Glancing at the map I knew the Thames path was not far away but my cycling sat nav has a feature you can use to direct you to the start of your new route. This lead to the day's cycling guest's cycling top tip.

Cycling guest cycling top tip 19. To avoid adding unnecessary miles and time to your ride don't just blindly follow your navigator's cycling sat nav when you clearly know it is taking you in completely the wrong direction.

Big George kept pointing out that I was clearly ignoring cycling guest cycling top tip 19 and started getting frustrated with my route. After a bit of a detour we eventually found the Thames cycle path, which runs along the side of the Thames for 20 uninterrupted traffic-free miles.

We whizzed along the bank past the O2 and Thames Barrier into a more industrial setting with cranes, jetties and unpleasant smelling chemical plants but all the time the Thames was giving us a dramatic and often picturesque view.

After a couple of hours we approached the final Thames path stretch before having to head inland through Dartford and under the M25 again. I persuaded Big George to be Boris one more time so I passed him the mask and was able to tweet a picture of the former Mayor waving me on my way after our London adventure.

With the light starting to fade the final few miles were far less pretty as, still on cycle paths, the route went alongside several busy roads (including the M2) as it wove its way to Gravesend.

Here we found the ferry jetty and, with the sun setting over Tilbury docks, we waited for the ferry to take us across the river and back to the car.

Setting off for Norwich Big George switched on his car sat nav and then ignored cycling guest cycling top tip No.19 himself as he allowed it to take us back on a route which added over half an hour to the journey.

*****

March was proving to be a good month with solid blog viewing figures but not the big numbers I had been hoping for. Surprisingly, the Boris bike ride hadn't captured the public's imagination so it was back to basics.

The March rides came thick and fast in number if rather dull in nature. During this time, one phenomenon I was regularly noticing was the confusion over meal times in the modern café era. I found that, despite normally arriving for my cafe stop well past midday, a large proportion of the average clientele would be tucking into a full English breakfast. When I was a lad breakfast was the meal you had to start the day, it had to be done and dusted by 9.00 and was usually oat or wheat based. Maybe at weekends you would be offered a fry up as a treat. It looks like times have changed and breakfast is now just another menu item rather than a mealtime in its own right. One could argue that cake and scones are teatime fare and shouldn't be eaten for lunch either, but let's not go there. I was increasingly worried that the Fry up Inspector's blog was having too much influence and I needed to redouble my efforts to push healthy cycling and cake up the agenda.

Chapter 29
(Visits 22,541 only 27,459 to go)

Now that spring was here it was time to return my focus to world record attempts and take mine to the next level. I wanted to undertake it shortly before Barry's deadline to give me one last push towards my goal. Before then I still had much to learn and the only way to do that was via some practice rides. To get me back on track I planned a 100-mile 10-café trip. This would help me develop the best route while I gathered useful data. I was still not confident that it was possible to eat a lot of cake when cycling a long way without being sick so this was a high-risk fact-finding ride.

I first checked the seven rules of calorie neutral bike riding that I had put in place last year after the Guinness book of records washed their hands of me. The ride needed to be as near to the real thing as possible so I would be cycling as fast as I could, stopping at each café to consume the requisite number of calories as quickly as I could.

I spent several minutes working out a route and timings, which I documented on an expertly prepared schedule ready for the ride.

The schedule suggested that I set off at 8:30 for my first cafe stop, an old favourite, the imaginatively named The Café at Brooke. It was a hard start to the day, as I had to climb the mountainous ridge over Poringland before hurtling down the Bungay Road to Brooke. I burnt 42 more calories than necessary, which as per rule 7 was wasted effort.

When I arrived at The Cafe there was no one about so I decided to save time and not lock the bike before dashing inside to order my first cake and drink of the day. I was wearing my bright yellow Hi-Viz gilet and stood patiently at the counter waiting to be served by the lady in the kitchen. After a couple of minutes, she came over apologising "oh sorry I didn't see you there" she said. My bright yellow Hi-Viz gilet clearly didn't live up to the 'make sure you are always seen' slogan promised in the advertising literature.

With precious minutes lost I went outside to eat my brownie and drink my hot chocolate (both very good) and see where I was against the printed schedule I had expertly prepared for the ride. This led to the first learning of the day, which was not to leave the printed schedule you had expertly prepared on your desk at home. Without it I would have no idea if I was reaching all my stops on time so I just had to go as fast as possible and hope for the best. To cheer me up I decided to take evidential photos of venue, drink and cake from each stop. To my horror, despite charging my phone the previous evening, it was already showing low battery. This meant my plans for regular Twitter updates were not going to happen either.

I gulped down the rest of my hot chocolate and with a burnt mouth I paid the lady who commented that I had been quick (yes less than 12 and a half minutes actually, thanks for asking) but I didn't have time to explain why as I set off for the next stop at Loddon.

Unfortunately, things didn't go to plan. As per rule 6 more than 300 calories need to be burnt between cafes. For some reason, cafes in this country are not spread out exactly 300 calories apart. To make sure I obey the rule it was sometimes necessary to put in extra loops and twists before arriving at each destination. To speed things up and avoid the time-consuming need to refer to maps, I had pre-loaded the route on to my bike sat nav. All I then had to do was follow the line on the display and I couldn't go wrong, or could I? As I arrived at one junction the sat nav showed the route line going both ways but no clue as to which was the right direction. I guessed wrong and a couple of miles later realised I had missed cafe number two altogether. There was no time to turn around so I pressed on to cafe number three, Every Day's a Picnic (EDAP) at Hedenham.

Now in a bit of a flap I was at least thankful that I had found a second café to stop at. I parked up my bike and headed inside.

Recently a friend of mine had been to EDAP and had been asked if she would like to try their award-winning cake only to discover the award was my Cake Crusader cake of the year and they had put up the certificate I made them on the wall.

I decided against having any award-winning chocolate Guinness cake on this ride, as it was a bit rich for my current needs, so instead I had a lovely piece of apple cake and some tea.

You may remember that when I did my five-cafe practice last autumn I discovered that it was not possible to drink more than four hot chocolates in one day without feeling sick. Instead I planned to have a hot chocolate at every fifth cafe and drink tea the rest of the time. My first tea of the day was provided in a nice pot with cup and saucer. As I was not used to tea drinking I wasn't sure if I was meant to drink just a cup worth or the full pot. To avoid the need for arbitration I decided to add a subsection to calorie neutral bike ride rule 5 that in these circumstances you only had to drink a single cup of tea.

Even if I had had my printed schedule, after missing out a cafe it would no longer have been of any use. Therefore after a brief (13.5 mins) and pleasant visit to EDAP I had no idea how I was doing. Undeterred I set off to Cake Crusader cafe of the year, Earsham Street cafe in Bungay. It was a straight-forward ride and again, as the cafe wasn't yet busy, service was quick. I sat out the back with my bike and enjoyed my cup of tea plus the most outstanding piece of cake of the day, which was Pear and Almond with chocolate bits. With cake this good it could be my number one rated cafe for some time to come.

After just under 14 mins of cake heaven it was once again time to get back on the bike. As I was leaving I noticed in the window that my café of the year certificate was proudly on display. Clearly my awards had been a hit in the local café community.

Next was a long pull west across to the Pennoyer centre in Pulham St Mary. With the wind, directly behind this was the fastest leg of the trip but it was also unnecessarily long, burning wasted world record calories and adding an unnecessary delay. There was clearly an opportunity to further optimise my world record route.

At the Pennoyer Centre I had my first cheese scone of the day, which through force of habit, I foolishly asked to be warmed wasting more valuable time. I was joined at my table by a local author who had read about my trip via a tweet on the Pennoyer centre website. It was exciting to meet my first ever calorie neutral bike ride supporter. He told me about the political novel he was writing, which sounded very interesting, but he had been wondering if I hadn't anything better to do with my time. He promised to look out for me on my actual attempt at the end of the summer which was very nice, especially if he made a flag to wave (which he didn't).

Next it was a ride north up to the Tudor Bakehouse in Long Stratton where there was further world record controversy. Being a bakery as well as a café, the Tudor Bakehouse had a good selection of muffins, biscuits, flapjacks and slices. Rule 4 clearly states that at each stop a cake or a scone must be consumed but no biscuits or flapjacks. I decided to go for the rather good-looking toffee tiffin. As I started to eat it I wondered if it was more biscuit than cake. When I returned home I checked the Wikipedia definition which says that tiffin is cake-like, composed of crushed biscuits and a layer of chocolate (or toffee) to hold it together and unlike regular cake it doesn't require baking. On reflection, I fear tiffin is neither cake nor scone so I broke rule 4. If today had been the world record attempt I would have been disqualified. To avoid any chance of this happening I amended rule 4 to be clear that tiffin is another food option not allowed.

Back on the bike I headed west to The Hen House near Wymondham, another award-winning café, this time for best atmosphere and ambiance (AAA). I really hoped that my home-made certificate would be on display there too. I was not disappointed as,

171

on arrival, not only was owner Annabel expecting me, via my tweets about the practice ride, but she had her certificate on display as well!

There was no time to soak up the award-winning AAA and once I had gulped down drink and cake it was straight back on the bike to Chalfonts at Hingham where I received some positive news.

The leg went smoothly as again the wind was in my favour so I arrived in good spirits as I locked my bike and went inside. Once I had sat down I checked my heart rate watch to discover I had only burnt 285 calories since the last cafe which broke rule six. Even though I was averaging well over 300 calories per stop rule 7 avoids any ambiguity so if this had been the real event I would have been disqualified, again. It was turning into calorie neutral cafe bike ride amateur night.

I decided not to get back on my bike and do the missing 15 calories but chalk it up as another learn and have some tea and cake instead. Chalfonts have a good selection of large cakes but it was against rule four to ask for a smaller slice, as a standard portion must be consumed. I went for the carrot cake as that looked like the smallest but it was still a very generous piece.

I had been here twice before but never managed to find out the opening times as they are not on display or on a website. I needed to know for world record route planning so today I asked the waitress and discovered they stayed open until 7.00pm on a Thursday and Friday. She also assured me they serve you right up to closing time, which, as I would find out later, is not always the case at every establishment. Excellent news, as I had been struggling to find enough cafes open past 5.00pm and I was going to need several to be able to hit my world record target of 20 cafes in a day. The only problem was that the ride was planned for a Tuesday. I decided that to give me the best chance of success the world record attempt would now be on a Friday in September.

After leaving Hingham it was a straightforward loop out to the Kings Cafe in Shipdham for hot chocolate and cake. While there I decided to try and fit another cafe in to replace the one I missed earlier in Loddon. It would mean a detour back to Wymondham but I felt there was still enough time. First I used up some of the 'only for emergencies' battery on my phone to check my cafe cycle spreadsheet which suggested that the Garden Tea rooms would be my best bet. From here on in, the remaining 20 miles of the route was going to be into the wind so I would have to work hard to get two more stops in before closing time.

When I arrived at the Garden Tea rooms the whole of Wymondham was closing so not surprisingly I was their only customer. I opted for a cheese scone with my pot of tea. Even though I knew it was very wrong I declined the offer of having my scone heated and had it cold for the sake of time. It was a very good cheese scone so it could comfortably carry off the lack of warmth.

With nine cafes down, I still had 45 minutes to make the final eight miles to Stephanie's coffee house near Crusader Towers, before their advertised 5.00pm closing time. Although directly into the wind, feeling a little delicate after so much tea and cake, and having already cycled 88 miles I still managed a good speed and arrived with what I thought was ten mins to spare. Unlike at Chalfonts in Hingham, Stephanie's did not serve up to the advertised closing time and I was greeted with the news that they had just stopped and it was drinking up time only now. Despite the extra effort I had put in I was unable to get my 10th cafe of the day visited.

A little downhearted I rode the short distance home and slumped on the sofa. Although I had failed to complete the ride as planned I was pleased that I had learnt many things and had much lovely new data to plan my final route and timings with.

I had an even clearer set of calorie neutral bike ride rules and regulations so I updated points four and five for clarity.

4. At each cafe a standard portion of cake or a scone (fruit or cheese) must be consumed. Biscuits, flapjacks, **tiffin** or anything pre-packaged will not count.
5. At each cafe a standard hot drink must be consumed. (Tea, coffee or hot chocolate). **If served in pot or jug than one cup must be drunk.**

I put all the data from my cycling computer into an overly complicated spreadsheet and looked at the facts. Although it would be difficult to plan the logistics I now believed 20 cafes might just be possible and a worthy target.

*****

I was starting to feel more confident about the world of café cycling, but then I discovered that one of my key regular cycling guests was no longer on board.

It all started innocently enough when I had arranged to go on a ride with Big George.

The trip was going to be a double whammy. First, because of my recent calorie neutral world record bike practice ride, I had decided that I needed to include a stop in Harleston to optimise my planned route. Secondly, I had recently started another project to go to a cafe named No 1 to No 100 until I had the full set. So far, I had done No 7 and No 51 meaning that this project was only in its infancy and I would need to pick up the pace if it was ever to be completed. So, when I discovered there was a cafe called No 5 in Harleston it was too good an opportunity to miss.

When Big George arrived, I could tell something was up. Rather than a cheery hello he just grunted. As the ride continued in silence I eventually plucked up courage and asked him if anything was wrong. After a long pause blurted out that he had become increasingly unhappy about the way he was being portrayed on the blog. He felt I had challenged his macho image by suggesting he had a passion for housework and often struggles at the end of our rides. He had decided that if I didn't write about him in a more 'accurate' light, then he would he would stop coming on our rides.

I was shocked, especially as I prided myself on the accuracy of my posts. Big George said I hoped I would see sense and advised me that he would not talk to me about dusting, hoovering or ironing so we exchanged superficial small talk on the way to Harleston.

We found No 5 on the main road that runs through the town. Big George had decided not to pander to any cake reviewing nonsense and to have something more Scottish and unhealthy instead as he asked for a fried egg sandwich on white bread with no garnish, which is clearly not cake. His loss I thought.

Despite this deliberately provocative action I was not to be put off my normal reviewing pattern and completed my spreadsheet with my views only, although I did deduce what Big George thought of his cappuccino so the hot guest drink quality (HGDQ) rating could be completed.

On the way back, it was obvious that Big George was very pleased with himself and felt his tactics were clearly starting to restore his macho image. With his guard down, I managed to extract from him his plans for the rest of the day. To recover from the ride, he was going to spend the afternoon in a nice relaxing bath using his favourite bath salts, and there may be just a few scented candles involved too. As Big George was a key player in my forthcoming plans I hoped that our differences would be quickly sorted out.

Surprisingly, after I had written up the post of the ride, Big George said he was not prepared to back down, as he claimed not to have used the scented candles for his bath after all. I decided the best plan was to invite him to be my cycling guest on a ride a week later to see if we could sort out our differences.

As we set off I decided to test the water so I asked him if he had any housework to do after the ride. He refused to answer this innocent question and produced a list of topics he was going to answer questions on and housework was not one of them. He handed over the list.

With few suitable topics available we continued in silence until we arrived at today's target venue 'The Sticky Bun', which turned out to be more cafe than tea room in style and I was again saddened to see there were plenty of customers still finishing their full English Breakfasts despite it being nearly lunchtime.

I went to check out the cakes and was disappointed that despite the café's name there were no buns, sticky or otherwise, and felt this was a missed opportunity by the Sticky Bun branding and marketing team.

As anything to do with cake was not on Big George's list of things we could talk about he deliberately didn't order any cake and once again went for a plain egg sandwich, on white no garnish, which was included on his list as an acceptable conversational area.

Luckily coffee was on his topics list and once we had depleted any egg sandwich-based chat he was at least prepared to rate his filter coffee for me.

By the time we set off the icy atmosphere had started to defrost and I was more hopeful that normal service maybe resumed. With conversation back on Big George told me about the rugby club u18s tour on which he was accompanying his son at the weekend. Rugby is top of his list of appropriate topics so no problem there. However, I was surprised to hear that as the tour was to Nottingham it was Robin Hood –themed and Big George was very excited to be able to go in fancy dress especially as he would be able to wear green tights for the whole trip. Fancy dress didn't sound like something that corresponded to his macho image agenda. I assumed this meant I could add fancy dress, Robin Hood and green tights to the bottom of the acceptable topics of conversation list for our next ride.

Despite the threat of losing Big George as a cycling guest, overall it had been a good month with the most rides and my highest blog figures to date. Still well short of the monthly numbers I needed to win the bet, but things were looking up. It was therefore time once again to meet up with Barry and share the good news.

Chapter 30
(Visits 25,367 only 24,623 to go)

I contacted Barry to see about a ride. I wanted to inform him that I was now halfway to my target, albeit having used up over three quarters of my time. He told me that Helen (new knee) and their Tandem (new replacement worn out parts) were both currently undergoing repairs so would be unable to join us but he was more than happy to come along as today's cycling guest.

With Barry's Tandem in the local bike shop I suggested Barry borrow one of my road bikes for a change. He agreed to give it a go but was distinctly unimpressed with the saddle that came with it. Barry explained that his bikes had far more comfortable seats featuring padding, gel and springs which he thought were preferable to the streamlined lightweight saddle that my spare modern road bike came with.

Due to the high winds, we kept the ride short and were pleased with the decision when we turned a corner and hit the wind head on, nearly coming to an immediate stop. We continued to battle through the gale for some miles during which I asked Barry how he was finding the bike in these conditions. Instead of telling me about the bicycle's excellent handling, the responsive feel of the carbon/alloy frame or the superior acceleration, he just said his bum hurt.

We made it through the worst of the wind but on crossing the foot bridge over the dual carriage way into Wymondham, Barry hit the kerb and came crashing down. Before I had a chance to act he got back to his feet clearly unhurt, but this led to today's cycling guest cycling top tip.

Cycling guest cycling top tip No. 23. To avoid your cycling host getting cross when you crash the bike he has kindly lent you, make sure you stay on the ground until after he has had a chance to take a photo of the incident for his cafe cycle blog.

I was more than a little annoyed, perhaps even fuming, that Barry had not followed cycling guest cycling top tip No 23.

By the time we got to Wymondham I had managed to calm down and find the Station Bistro, which, by coincidence, was next to Wymondham railway station.

While I went to check out the cake selection Barry went to test that the chairs were going to be comfortable enough for him to sit on. As always Barry had a sausage roll, which is not a cake, but to show willing he compromised by also having some chocolate biscuit cake. It looked good although I'm not convinced you can be both a biscuit and a cake at the same time. He confirmed that the chairs met his high bottom comfort criteria standards.

Just in time, our large collection of drinks and food arrived. I tried to engage Barry in the latest blog stats but he wasn't listening as a train was pulling into the station. When I eventually got Barry's attention away from the trains I told him the latest stats and the good growth I had had. He quickly did the math and pointed out that I was still nowhere close to his internet sensation target before going back to observing the train action out on the platform. I knew he was right but felt I still had enough tricks up my sleeve to pull it off, especially if the world record attempt could attract some media attention, which up to now it had not.

*****

It was clear where my focus needed to be, so once again I turned my attention to the calorie neutral café ride world record attempt. Despite having undertaken my two practice runs, it was all still a bit haphazard and would not be professional enough for the media coverage I needed.

Up to now most of my time had been spent on planning the start of the ride, so I thought it was now time to test out the route of the potential last eight cafes. I felt I had got the preparation right for once but in the end this pilot run made me look even more the world record amateur than before.

One of the major issues I had experienced was getting any consistency on counting the calories between cafes. Rather fundamental to a calorie neutral bike ride so I would also be refining calorie neutral bike ride world record attempt rule 6.

Rule 6. From the time of arriving at the cafe 300 calories must be burnt off before the next cafe can be visited thus making the ride calorie neutral. (300 calories are based on in-depth internet research on average calories of cakes and scones plus average calories of a hot drink (Tea, coffee, hot chocolate).

Using the data from my previous two practice rides I had developed an optimised route for today's target cafes in order that the minimum distance would be needed between stops when burning the necessary 300 calories. As always, I was using my Garmin Forerunner 910XT, with a heart rate monitor, to measure the calories.

With GPS route programmed, notebook and calorie counter all in place, I set off, before breakfast, to the start point for the day. On this ride, I would only be stopping if I felt I was running out of energy as today it was all about tuning the route in line with actual calorie count.

With the wind behind I was soon at the end of the drive to the Hen House café, where I planned to begin today's data-gathering activity.

I knew the roads round here well and therefore had no difficulty in finding my way to the first stop, which was Lincoln's Tea Shoppe in Hingham. I was confident that I had pedalled just the right number of miles necessary to shift the correct calories. On arrival, I stopped and checked my calorie count readout. I was shocked and mystified to find I had only burnt 223 calories, 67 calories short of my target.

Disappointed, I made a note to add a couple more miles on to the route and set off again.

Next cafe on the list was Tabnabs in Mattishall, which was once again a trip on familiar roads. I was particularly enjoying being out in the Norfolk countryside without the pressure of doing another café review for once. My good mood soon changed though, as when checking my calorie count at Tabnabs I again found I was many calories short. If every cafe required an extra couple of miles then the 20 cafe target I had set would not be possible. I was now both puzzled and dejected as I set off for test stop number three.

I did consider abandoning the practice ride at this point but I decided to keep going and cycle to the next stop, Yaxham Mill Cafe Bar, as I was now rather hungry and ready for breakfast.

Despite this not being a cafe reviewing ride, force of habit took over and I found myself taking a photograph of the breakfast (cheese scone and hot chocolate) before I realised I had done it. The refreshments were very good and replaced some of the tiny number of calories I had apparently burned.

Next was a loop round to Yaxham Waters café. I tried going a bit slower to see if that helped but it seemed to make no difference with the pattern of not enough calories repeated and it was the same story on the way to Chalfonts in Hingham.

The day had not turned out as planned and it was looking like a major rethink would be needed. In fact, if today's findings were to be used, I would either have to get my cycling up to Olympic standard or do a rather unremarkable number of cafes which would then be unlikely to generate the blog publicity that this activity was all about.

Totally deflated, it was time for the longest leg of the day from Hingham to Janey's village cafe in Hethersett. By the time I got there I had covered over 50 miles and had only had a cheese scone and hot chocolate to keep me going so I decided it was time for a calorie top-up.

I ordered another hot chocolate plus carrot cake, to make sure I got some vegetables inside, as I know the importance of a balanced diet. As I waited for them to arrive I noticed that this was the only time all day that I had hit my calorie target and had overshot it by nearly one hundred. This made no sense at all as I had only gone a couple of miles further than the distances between the other cafes. I was now starting to suspect my Garmin's calorie counting abilities.

I was pleased that the carrot cake was a generous (and tasty) slice, which, like a Pavlovian dog with an i-phone, I had photographed before I knew it.

Now fully recharged I hopped back on my bike for the ride to the last stop of the route, the Station Bistro in Wymondham (with another insufficient calorie count).

Data recording was over so I set off home to try and make sense of my findings. Once back in my secret underground bicycle workshop at Crusader Towers I updated all the data into my computer which showed, according to my Garmin Forerunner 910XT, I was now operating at much lower calories per mile than on the previous two practice rides.

I was at a loss to know what to make of it all. I decided to hand all the data over to some boffins so they could crunch the numbers in a super computer and come up with the definitive answer as to how far I need to cycle between cafes to burn 300 calories.

They quickly reported back and confirmed that my Garmin forerunner 910XT was probably not recording enough calories due to an inaccurate heart rate monitor. Their conclusion was that I only needed to do about 5 miles or 20 mins cycling to burn the 300 calories at my target 15mph speed. Calorie counting without a heart rate monitor would give a more consistent result.

This was good news, although I would have to do the route again on this basis with no heart rate monitor to confirm the findings. A meaningful world record attempt was back on.

For clarity, I added a new rule, 8, about calorie counting equipment

8. **Calories burnt to be counted on a generic calorie counting device using only cycle speed, rider weight and age to calculate calorie usage. No heart rate consideration is required.**

Chapter 31
(Visits 26,211 only 23,789 to go)

The world record attempt wasn't for a few months but I wanted to maximise the publicity opportunities to get the obvious increase in visitor numbers that such a momentous activity was sure to generate. But how?

I couldn't put all my eggs in one basket so I also had two new ideas for attracting more readers. Talking of eggs, I decided to try and cram my Twitter Egg News feature into my now bulging bad ideas drawer. I had noticed that after every egg-based tweet, including photos, I would lose some of my dwindling Twitter followers. It was scaring people off so I decided that the world was clearly not yet ready for such innovation.

New idea one was to go back to Europe to cycle up some mountains. This would not only attract more alpine readers but I would see how cake performs at altitude. To date my European adventures had not attracted high numbers but I felt it was worth the risk, especially as I would also be able to return to the Hotel Vitranc in Slovenia which had won the European café of the year certificate the previous year. It would give me the opportunity to present it in person and maybe attract some local media interest.

My second idea had come about as I realised that my blog was rather Norfolk-biased and I wanted to attract a wider national audience. I thought that the best way to do this was find the best café across Great Britain. In that way I would really have gone national, in a big way. Clearly, I didn't have time to go to every café across Great Britain but instead I came up with a clever solution to get around this particular logistical challenge.

I reckoned that if I cycled from St David's in Wales (the furthest point west) to Lowestoft (the furthest point east) I would be cycling across Great Britain. I then only had to decide which café was the best one en-route and I would have found the best café across Great Britain, literally.

The other good news was that Big George was back on side after I promised to show him in a better light on the blog and he promised not to read it. He told me he had some exciting media news so we met.

I was pleased that normal conversation could be resumed but less pleased when he informed me the media news was about him and not the blog. It transpired that he had been on BBC Radio 5 live the previous week. I assumed he had phoned in but he told me he had been invited on as a guest in a debate on education in Norfolk. As it was getting near local election time BBC Radio 5 live had come to Norwich that week. Apparently one of the producers was an old friend of Big George's so had lined him up to be on a panel talking about education because when Big George is not out cycling with me, or doing the housework, he teaches.

As I started to glaze over he gave me a blow by blow account of what he had said, plus what he should have said when he thought about it later, what the other debaters had said and how he believed his contribution would impact the result of the elections. He was very proud that he had made two contributions. I asked if he had managed to mention the blog but was disappointed that he had not found a way to bring it up.

Another golden media opportunity had been missed, I thought, but then a couple of days later, out of the blue, I got an email from Anglia TV. It simply said
"Can you give me a little call - I'd like to make a little film about you!!"

This was what I had been waiting for. It was a shame it would only be a little film and not a weekly series but it was a start and I had got two exclamation marks which looked really positive.

I immediately phoned the number and got put straight through to an answer phone where I left an appropriate message and waited for the world of television to come to me.

Six weeks later I had still heard nothing so sent a follow up e-mail asking if she was still interested in making the film which generated the following reply.

"I AM but they keep putting me on grisly court cases and inquests. I am next in on Tuesday let me discuss and get back to you. I am sorry for the delay".

My hopes were raised again, so I sat back and looked forward to next Tuesday when I expected to receive the film's story board and further instructions.

While waiting for my debut on the small screen I had been distracted as I had entered an Ironman triathlon at the start of summer and to be ready for that I needed to increase the amount of cycling I was doing although none of the training plans I had read suggested stopping during your cycle training to eat cakes and scones. However, I still planned to fit in at least one cafe cycle ride each week where cake would form part of that day's nutrition plan.

The blog now seemed to have attracted some traction as café and teashop owners sometimes contacted me requesting a visit. I was therefore very pleased to be presented with an opportunity to attract a potentially new demographic to the blog, The Lady Who Shops.

I had been invited to visit a tearoom named Tea, Bags and Shoes. Their establishment is not just a tearoom but sells ladies' shoes and bags as well. I therefore foolishly invited Mrs Crusader to be my cycling guest as I thought she would appreciate the bags and shoes more than me, with the inevitable consequence.

The ride had gone well and we soon found ourselves at the target destination. Tea, Bags and Shoes is part of a set of shops set some way back from the main road. You get to the tearoom part of the shop through the bag and shoe bit. I made it straight through with little difficulty but Mrs Crusader got distracted on the way. She had still not turned up by the time I had rated the effective cake selection and sat down ready to order.

Mrs Crusader finally made it to our table while I was waiting for some fresh cheese scones to be baked, but before I had time for in depth cake reviewing she had gulped down her drink, shoved her cake into her mouth and disappeared back into the shoe part of the shop like a magpie attracted to shiny things.

Soon the cheese scones were ready but the table behind me got theirs first as they had been waiting longer having finished off the scones from the original batch. Mrs Tea, Mrs Bags or Mrs Shoe (I never did find out which) suggested they should compare the batches. "We could score them out of ten" they laughed. What a ridiculous thing to do, I thought.

My cheese scone soon followed and was obviously warm, as it was straight out of the oven, it was also very nice so I could now give an overall cake taste quality rating (CTQ), out of ten.

While all the cheese scone action had been going on Mrs Crusader had tried some new shoes on as she had apparently discovered a gap in her current shoe collection that could be successfully filled with some new smart green boots. When pressed I of course said that they were very nice, which was all the encouragement she needed. Before I knew it, she was demanding I hand over all my spare cafe cycle pocket money allowance, to make up the shortfall in the cash she had on her. I reluctantly handed it over, knowing that as one shoe gap is filled another one soon opens.

Tea, Bags and Shoes had scored well although I suspect that it would score even higher with those who understood the Bags and Shoes part of the proposition.

On the way home Mrs Crusader started to plan the new clothes she would need to go with the new shoes. Thank goodness, I have so far not found a combined tearoom and ladies clothes shop (at least not one I am ever likely to visit).

Judging by the response to the post, ladies who shop don't cycle to cafes and tearooms. Worse still my blog visitor numbers were showing no sign of the exponential growth required although they were hitting a solid 2000 a month which at least showed there was some interest in my work. The same couldn't be said of my Twitter followers, most of whom seemed to be small businesses hoping I would follow them if they followed me. I decided not to stoop to their level and hoped they would stay with me because of my "amusing and informative" tweets.

To encourage this, I started a café and cycling Q&A service on Twitter where I would use my new-found expertise to answer people's questions. Which is quite hard in 142 characters but I did my best

- Burt says it's not safe to listen to my iPod when riding any ideas? Simply hum a tune, if you want to switch tracks hum another tune instead
- Alan of Hingham has asked, I know it's cheese scone hot, fruit scone not but what about plain ones. Well Alan, plain scone warm, is the norm
- Bill from Ely says I keep coming second in bike time trials, any tips to get me that extra zip needed to win. Bill, try to pedal a bit faster
- Clive of Diss asks, I was arguing with my wife about whether scone is pronounced scone or scone. Which is it? Well Clive, it's scone
- Colin writes, when on a ride if overtaken by someone a. Bigger, b. On a worse bike, c. Older should you chase after them? Yes, it's compulsory

- Kim from Ely asks, I'm about to do some baking any tips? Yes, make sure you buy plenty of scratch as everything can be made by starting from it
- Ken from Woodbridge wants to know what the best way of avoiding punctures is. I suggest you don't ride over sharp things
- John from Thetford is worried about his dog chasing anything on a bike. John, to avoid further problems simply confiscate the dog's bike.
- Sid asks what is the best way to boil an egg? Pop it in boiling water, hop on your bike riding at exactly 20mph. After a mile the egg will be done
- Liz from Sandringham wants to know if there is a way of taking her Corgi with her on a bike ride. I suggest popping it in a small backpack.
- Ted from Poringland has asked what I do if I plan to go on a ride and then it rains. Ted, I get wet.
- Tim wants to avoid getting a sore behind. I suggest a naan bread on your saddle. Makes ride comfortable & when you get home a warm snack.

I ran the feature daily for several weeks, making up the questions as well as the answers while I waited for people to start to tweet me real ones (they never did) and eventually I ran out of ideas with little increase in followers.

Chapter 32
(Visits 27393 only 22607 to go)

As I approached the start of my next cycling experiment, to see how cafes up mountains perform compared with those nearer sea level, I needed to find a cycling guest up to the task. Fortunately, Andrew is a sucker for anything Italian so, on the promise that Italian mountains would be included on the itinerary, he agreed to join me.

Intrinsic to the plan was the need to cycle up lots of steep climbs, and there aren't any available in Norfolk, so I decided to take Andrew on a couple of long training rides for preparation as I suspected he wouldn't have done any himself. During both these sessions, he once again demonstrated just how notoriously hard to please he was which should have been a warning for what was to come once abroad.

The café on the first trip was at Creake Abbey. On arrival we went inside to the spacious indoor seating area and sat down to order. As it was lunch time we both ordered a cheese sandwich to go with our hot drinks and cake. I had been attracted to this particular sandwich on the menu as it came with chilli jam, which I'm particularly fond of. Andrew is not only notoriously hard to please but exceptionally bad at making decisions. Therefore, he just copied me and asked for the cheese sandwich as well, Andrew then asked the waitress if she could tempt him with an alternative to chilli jam as he doesn't like it.

She thought for a moment and then suggested they could add a nice chutney. A good offer I thought but Andrew declined. She then said a relish would be nice but he didn't like the sound of that either so said he would have it plain.

After the waitress had gone I asked him what he was hoping to be offered instead of chilli jam and he said "salad".

I was puzzled, "If you knew what you wanted, why didn't you just ask for some salad rather than try and make the poor waitress guess?" I asked.

He told me that he could have done that but felt it was part of the waitress role to understand and anticipate the customer's needs and he would rather forgo the salad than let her off the hook. When the cheese sandwiches turned up they came with a salad and coleslaw garnish anyway. Maybe his customer needs had been fully anticipated and understood or maybe the sandwiches just came with salad.

It had been a long ride and we had kept up a good speed so I was happy, and surprised, that Andrew was getting into shape for our forthcoming trip, but just to make sure I organised another long ride soon after. Although the ride went well he again he demonstrated his peculiar food ordering approach as I returned to Wortham Tea rooms.

As usual we took our seats and ordered our cakes and hot drinks. As he was peckish Andrew also ordered an omelette, asking the friendly and patient waitress what fillings he could have. She proudly told him they had virtually any filling you can think of. You could see the cogs whirling in his head as he weighed up the multitude of opportunities before eventually coming up with cheese. Obviously disappointed with his rather predictable and conservative choice she returned to the kitchen to put in our order. I asked Andrew why he hadn't gone for something more challenging but he said he only likes cheese omelettes.

On the way back, despite the lack of mountains, we started preparing for our trip to the Slovenian Alps in more detail. Andrew told me to text him with a list of anything he might have forgotten to pack.

The two training rides plus my excellent packing list meant that I was confident Andrew was in good shape and had packed everything when he turned up at Crusader Towers the following week, ready for the trip to the airport and our Alpine adventure.

*****

In terms of blog visitor numbers, it was apparent that my regular readers appeared to prefer a shorter ride as the longer ones I had recently been doing were attracting fewer people. This did not bode well for cycling trips half way across Europe especially as previous trips abroad had always flopped but I was hopeful that this time I would hit the European tipping point.

We had an incident-free trip over to our alpine base camp in Kransjka Gora on the Slovenian, Italian, Austrian border. One additional advantage of the trip would be my final chance for cycle training before my Ironman triathlon event. I had heard that training at high altitude was very good for you so this trip should bring my fitness up to scratch. Base camp was at only 810m, which apparently isn't very high in altitude training terms, but it is a lot higher than Norfolk so it would have to do.

The first ride was three climbs and 65 miles that should get us into the right high-altitude mindset. So, after a muesli-based breakfast we headed straight up the iconic 11km ride to Vršič with its 24-hairpin bends, the most famous climb in the region.

Despite having two long flat training rides under his belt, Andrew was a bit nervous of how he would get on with such demanding terrain especially when I disappeared up the road. I go up quicker than Andrew so we were soon some way apart and knowing this would be the case had agreed to meet at the top. I hadn't got very far when I was asked to stop by a man in Hi-Viz. You should never disobey a man in Hi-Viz so I obediently stopped and politely enquired the reason for the delay. He told me that several coaches full of cycling fans needed to get by. I asked if there was a big race on today but he laughed and said they were just making a TV commercial featuring cycling and needed some pretend cycling fans.

Once allowed to set off again I rounded the corner to find the road lined with the pretend cycling fans practising their cheering. They were clearly very good pretend cycling fans as I found myself waving and punching the air as I cycled past. This had the desired effect as the pretend cycling fans started to cheer back, sound their hooters and wave their flags. In return I waved and air punched back even more. Andrew, who hates this sort of thing, was a little way behind me but by now I had whipped up the pretend cycling fans and I could now hear behind me that they were now cheering him too.

It was hard work but there were good views to be seen between the gaps in the trees helping to take my mind off my aching legs and lungs. It takes about an hour of constant uphill pedalling to reach the top but I was keen to do it without stopping. As I approached half way I went past a cafe and saw behind me an old bloke, wearing a checked shirt and some flannel trousers, pull out on his hybrid-style bike. He had clearly stopped for a rest so I expected that I would soon be leaving him far behind as I continued grinding my way up hill. After a while I looked round and to my horror found that he was catching me up. I was both impressed with how fit old people in Slovenia were and disappointed with my own obvious lack of form. I was sure he would fade so tried to pedal a bit harder in an attempt to distance him but as we went around each hairpin he was closing in. Although I was now on my last legs I dug deep and just beat him to the summit by a couple of bike lengths.

I collapsed by the summit picnic area exhausted but was happy that no old Slovenian cyclist, especially one in casual clothing, had beaten me up a mountain. I lay on the grass panting for breath and waited for Andrew when the old bloke wandered over and offered me some Slovenian sausage. He looked as fresh as a daisy and I now had huge respect for him so was about to accept his sausage gesture of friendship, when I realised he was riding a motor assisted electric bike. He was a cycling fraud and not the type of cyclist I would want to be seen with so I asked him to put away his patronising sausage and left him to get on with his ill-gotten picnic alone.

When Andrew eventually arrived, he asked if I had seen the man over there with the e-bike. I told him that I didn't know what he was talking about and suggested that we got on with the ride. From here it was now downhill for many miles. Whereas I'm a lot quicker uphill, Andrew is a lot quicker downhill so disappeared off into the distance as he whizzed around the 26-hairpin bends on that side of the mountain. It became apparent we did not make ideal cycling companions for the mountains as we didn't see each other again all morning.

When the road eventually flattened out we found ourselves in the beautiful Soca valley near the village of Bovec. Andrew had kindly waited for me while I caught up. However, we were now at the bottom again so, in the words of Yazz and the Plastic Population, the only way was up.

Before we started on the up again we stopped for lunch at The Encuan grill. It was more of a shed with a large outdoor seating area than the sort of tea room I was used to but it came with some dramatic views of the surrounding mountains. On the downside, we were surrounded by bikers of the full motorised variety. The only trouble with cycling in these parts is the number of bikers the area also attracts. They get a different pleasure out of the landscape by making the most of the winding roads seeming to think that they are like the corners on a grand prix racing track, which they are clearly not.

As usual for a trip outside the UK I was using the European cafe cycle review system which just rates drink, food and AAA. Drink options were limited although the food, gnocchi for me and Greek salad for Andrew, were very good but not good enough to challenge for the best café anywhere in Europe ever title.

Now refuelled we had much climbing still to do. It soon started up again as we found ourselves cycling apart. It was a shorter climb but still took the best part of an hour to complete. At the top was the old Slovenian Italian border crossing which meant I was now in Italy. I didn't wait for Andrew this time as I now knew he would catch up on the way down.

We eventually met up again and continued through Tarvisio in Italy all the way to the Italian Austrian border on an off-road cycle path through the woods. It was our third country of the day which meant it must have been time for my next cafe review.

The view didn't include mountains as it overlooked the deserted border crossing. Andrew decided he liked the deserted border crossing vibe and decided he might start his own cycling deserted border crossings blog and have all the photos in black and white to generate the right mood. Good luck with that, I thought.

Whilst enjoying our hot drinks and profiteroles, Andrew announced his lunchtime Greek salad was now causing him issues and popped off to sort himself out. He then made me reduce the high food score we had awarded at lunchtime.

With our second stop complete we set off for the final climb of the day back over to Slovenia, which meant a short ride in Austria before we reached the Wurzen pass. Once on the steep slopes we were soon separated and to make matters worse there were swarms of pesky motor bikes who continued to accelerate past us on every bend. This was not only the hardest climb of the day but hardest I have ever done, especially when I saw a sign saying it was 18%. My cycling GPS goes on auto pause if you go below a certain speed as it assumes you must be pushing your bike or stopped. It did this several times on the way up despite me keeping going all the way.

Even though it was the shortest climb of the day, it was still 15 minutes before Andrew appeared at the top and he did not seem in the best of moods. He immediately passed on today's cycling guest top cycling tip.

Cycling guest cycling top tip no 30. Never cycle up a hill with an 18% hill sign at the bottom but if you do make sure you re-plan any other such routes if you want to avoid doing those rides alone.

When we got back I compared our 65 miles and 2400m ascending with a typical Tour de France mountain stage to discover they go twice as far and twice as high in half the time (not including cafe stops) which sort of put our ride into perspective.

Later that evening we told the waiter in a local restaurant where we had gone he said, "you didn't want to do that, everyone else cycles that route the other way around as it's much easier". It didn't help Andrew's mood. I promised him a longer but flatter ride tomorrow but I had no idea if it really was although I did avoid going over the Wurzen pass again.

The main purpose of this trip was to find a really good European cycle café which might break the blog in Europe. Unfortunately, yesterday had produced some good, if not spectacular, fare so I was hoping for better today. To have more café opportunities the ride was going to be nearly 100 miles long. I had told Andrew that despite today's ride being 30 miles further, this was not a problem as we wouldn't be doing three tough climbs like yesterday. I did say it was just theory, based on looking at the map, but it also turned out to be a lie.

As it was going to be a long one we set off early at 8.00am and soon made it to the Slovenian/Italian border where we took the latest black and white photo for Andrew's potential deserted border crossings and cycling based blog. He felt this was the best one to date.

It was then a long straight section in Italy ready for our first climb of the day back to the Slovenian border and more deserted border crossing action (in black and white of course).

Up until now it had been very pleasant riding as we were not bothered by those annoying motor bikers. However, at the stroke of 10 o'clock out they all came, racing along in their sweaty leathers. It said it all, us cyclists get up at 7.00am have our muesli breakfast and are on the road by 8:00am while our motor biking 'friends' are getting up late, stuffing themselves full of fried things and croissants before unnecessarily spooking the poor cyclist with their pointless overtaking manoeuvres. They don't even stop to take black and white photos of deserted border crossings.

We crossed the border and headed down hill to Bovec again before we decided to stop for elevenses at Pro Mostu pizzeria.

It was a stunning view from the undercover terrace outside seating area where we ordered our refreshments. To go with Andrew's cappuccino and my hot chocolate I asked if they had any food. Yes, they did, I was told, but not yet as it was too early in the day. I asked if they had any cake or strudel but apparently, they ran out yesterday. This was a problem as European café cycle reviewing rules state that food must be rated for the café to qualify. The only food I could now rate was the tiny biscuit that came with the hot drinks. After much debate we awarded a generous 3.5 out of 10 for the food quality mark.

The views and atmosphere were first class but due to the poor biscuit score the overall rating was at the lower end of my European list and I didn't think I would see my blog punters rushing to read about it.

The waitress also explained that it was now peak biker season which, combined with the nice weather, meant that they were currently swarming like a plague of leather clad locusts.

Undeterred by yet another disappointing stop we continued to zig zag between Italy and Slovenia
and were soon on our second climb of the day which was on a very narrow and bumpy road gently winding up through the trees for

197

what seemed like forever. Although this wasn't the best of road conditions it had the definite advantage of putting off the bikers so for once we had it to ourselves.

As it was a very long steady climb I had once again left Andrew far behind but I was finding it tough going on such a hot day. So, when I saw a nice-looking cafe with a fantastic view I made the executive decision to stop for lunch at Baita al botton d'Ora cafe.

When Andrew eventually rode in I had nearly finished eating my Bolognese and drinking lots of bottled water. He sat down opposite and ignored me as he immediately ordered an espresso plus some gnocchi. The weather may have been hot but the atmosphere was rather frosty.

We had to put personal issues to one side as there was reviewing to be done so I moved the conversation on to that. In terms of atmosphere and ambiance (AAA) it was delightful with a fantastic view and proper Italian rustic charm plus no one spoke any English. Andrew (who is notoriously hard to please unless it has anything to do with Italy) wanted to give it 11 out of 10 which is clearly mathematical nonsense but I thought I needed to keep him keep him happy so I said I would, but obviously, I didn't.

The Baita al botton d'Ora cafe shot straight to the top of my 'Best European café ever' league in spite of there being no hot chocolate. But don't all rush there as it is hard to get to and I was sure that Europe could still do much better. This was my fourth trip to the continent in search of cafes but I still didn't think I had found a destination yet that delivered the cafe experience I was after.

Leaving the Baita al botton d'Ora we descended a very tricky road. By the end of this technical descent my hands were aching from pulling hard on the brakes but I eventually caught up with Andrew at the bottom.

The pattern of the trip was repeated as after some more flat we started to climb gently up again. I assured Andrew it would not be a steep climb but this turned out to be far from the truth as the longer we went the steeper it got. It took over an hour to go less than seven miles which is rather slow.

After we got to the top (15 mins apart as usual) it was another steep descent until we once again regrouped. I had decided not to wait for Andrew at the top in case he was rather angry about the amount of climbing I had made him do. This turned out to be a good plan as he told me he had had time to calm down on the descent and had decided not to kill me after all. Although I think I was safe as he would have been too tired to do it anyway.

The next part of the ride was on a lovely flat cycle path which went along an old railway line for several miles. We arrived at the point where I had planned to turn off for the final climb and cafe stop. I wasn't sure how to persuade Andrew to go up again as he looked in need of further refreshments and refuelling. But what was this? At the junction there was a cafe and information point.

I assumed it was a mirage but things only got better when the information lady told us we could continue along the cycle path all the way to back to Slovenia and there was no need to cycle over another mountain. Next, they provided excellent hot chocolate and cappuccino along with some lovely plum tart.

I sat there by the side of the world's best cycle path enjoying smashing refreshments and lapping up the fabulous views. I knew I had at last found a top quality continental cycle cafe which was now officially the best one anywhere in Europe ever.

I checked my watch and realised that we had been enjoying relaxing rather too much and bicycles don't cycle themselves (unless they are motorbikes and I think we know my opinion on that) so it was time to get going again as there were still over 30 miles to ride. Although the cycle path was smooth it had a gentle incline all the way so this part was tiring on the legs as they had to keep pedalling and on the ears as Andrew kept ranting. I informed both my legs and Andrew that this was a much quicker and easier option than the alternative would have been as I pointed to the high mountains on either side of the valley we were in.

When we got back I checked the ride statistics and discovered that we had cycled nearly 100 miles and been out on the road for 11 hours. I felt today had been a great success especially after finding the number one cafe in Europe and the miraculous cycle track. I'm not sure Andrew was convinced as he lay on the sofa refusing to move.

I told Andrew that we had in fact done more climbing metres than yesterday which seemed to make him both pleased and annoyed at the same time. He decided he would take more interest in the next day's route which I assured him was both shorter and flatter, but, as I had never actually ridden the route before it was only a theory and to date all my pre-route predictions had been very wrong. I just hoped he had enough strength to complete the last ride but as it turned out he didn't.

*****

Today's plan was to head to Austria where we could find a lake to cycle round. My theory was that lakes must get put somewhere flat to stop all the water running out. While there we would obviously check out the Austrian lakeside café scene before returning to Slovenia to revisit Hotel Vitranc, the European cafe of the previous year.

The only issue was we were in Slovenia and Austria was the other side of the dreaded Wurzen pass. Andrew was still refusing to go near it and had been moaning about how hard it was ever since riding up it. However, today we would be going the other way which is a much easier climb as you start from higher up in Slovenia.

Much to our surprise we reached the top with ease and I could take a deserted boarding crossing black and white photo from the opposite side for Andrew's potential new blog.

Going down again was the scariest experience of the trip as you can pick up a lot of speed on a hill that steep, and if it ends in a hairpin bend then it gets a bit tricky. We were not helped by our motor biking "friends" insisting on overtaking everything coming up the hill and heading straight for us. Needless to say, I had very sore hands and bottom from gripping both the brakes and my buttocks very tightly.

The ride round the lake itself proved disappointing as all the prime lakeside real estate was full of private houses meaning that although there was a good cycle path on the other side of them, you could only get the odd glimpse of the water.

Finding somewhere to review was not proving easy either. All the lakeside cafes we passed were either part of campsites, which Andrew refused to go near, or looked overly touristy, and Andrew hates tourists even more than campers. We then spotted the Urbani Wirt café on the other side of the road so decided to try there instead.

The cafe itself had a shady outside seating area with the only distraction being the nearby road. As a bonus the waiter and waitress wore traditional lederhosen to give an authentic feel and therefore a good AAA score was awarded.

After our stop, we continued to the far end of the lake and headed up into foothills which had a bit of climbing but nothing too difficult compared with our hour plus uphill experiences of the previous days. It was completely different scenery being much more open than on our proper mountain trips so hopefully more to Andrew's liking. So much so, in fact, that Andrew insisted on an unscheduled ten-minute break to "admire the view and soak up the scenery". Apparently, this is something called a rest. I had no idea why you would want to do this as it did not add to total miles, metres climbed or average speed stats, but I reluctantly agreed he could have five minutes whilst I twiddled my thumbs and looked at maps and data.

When we eventually set off again we were now on the south side of the lake and in search of a late lunch.

We chose to try cafe Gasthaus Messnai at Bade Strand as it had a lake view and wasn't too busy. When he took his seat in the outdoor seating area Andrew was annoyed to find his lake view was obscured by a fruit tree which he thought the cafe needed to cut down. I felt that moving his chair might be an easier option but he pointed out that it wasn't him who had placed the chair there in the first place and the customer is always right.

I was pleased that hot chocolate was available although the waitress was not so impressed with Andrew's food choice of salad and chips. Like me she was probably worried that salad and chips was not enough fuel for the remaining 40 miles of ride, especially in these temperatures and after he had already needed to do that funny rest thing earlier. It was no surprise when later that day she would be proved right.

Even though my hot chocolate looked anaemic it was quite nice as was Andrew's cappuccino. I had tortellini and chips for lunch which was also good so overall, despite the fruit tree issue and lack of lederhosen, it was another good cafe score.

There were no more hills to go over but as the temperature had risen to over 30c the rest of the ride was still hard work. With just six miles to go it was clear the mixed salad and chips had run out as Andrew did the unthinkable and asked if we could stop for another rest. I was forced to wait as Andrew collapsed off his bike like a rag doll and fell motionless to the ground.

Although he had stopped speaking he appeared to be breathing so I waited patiently for him to sit up and have some energy drink from his water bottle. After a few more minutes Andrew finally announced this overly dramatic rest was over and we could set off again on the final push to the Hotel Vitranc in Podkoren.

Cycling guest cycling top tip no 31 To enjoy a cycle ride without the need for unscheduled stops or rests then make sure you eat more than a mixed salad and chips for lunch.

Hotel Vitranc had been awarded European cafe of the previous year. I had emailed them their winner's certificate but surprisingly they had never responded to me about receiving such a prestigious award. It seemed like the easiest option was to bring a certificate out with me to hand over in person, which I was sure would cause much excitement.

Whilst we waited to find someone more senior than the waiter to give the certificate to I ordered a hot chocolate and strudel only to find they had run out of both. I went for pancakes instead. Andrew had another cappuccino and pancakes to help refuel.

The food and drinks were nice but due to lack of food options their new rating was well below my new favourite European café on the cycle path in Italy. As there was no one at reception and they had lost their top spot I decided to give the certificate to the waiter after all. As Andrew took a photo of the ceremony the bemused waiter thanked me and then said something in Slovenian. I had seen that expression before so assumed it was "Haven't you got anything better to do with your time". All a bit of an anti-climax.

After over 260 miles of cycling, including a lot of climbs, my backside was very happy to be travelling home with me rather than spending more time on the bike. I had regularly posted about the trip plus news of the new number one European café so I had high hopes that I would be getting a big boost in blog visitor numbers.

On checking the site count a few days later, I was disappointed to see my continental posts had again performed far worse than the standard rides in Norfolk. This was obviously not the way to go to become an internet sensation.

The key had to be better publicity so it was time to up my media campaign. My big hope, of appearing on local TV had gone nowhere as the lady from Anglia TV still hadn't got back. I decided I would have to get my people to speak to their people to see if we could get the deal back on. I dropped a quick email to her and she assured me that she would be in touch again very soon. Clearly, I was no longer big news. But then my luck changed.

Chapter 33
(Visits 29588 only 20412 to go)

I may have mentioned that I had been training to do an Ironman triathlon and the event was now not far away. As part of my training I had been a regular at the local parkrun on Saturday mornings. This week I had decided it was about time I volunteered to help with marshalling the event. As us volunteers waited for the event to start I was introduced to another of today's helpers called Sam. Nothing unusual about that until he said he was a journalist on the local paper (the Eastern Daily Press or EDP to its friends). Well this was too good an opportunity to miss and I subtly guided the conversation round to my blog suggesting that it would make a good article to help fill up the pages of his paper.

Much to my surprise he liked the idea and said he would run it past his editor before getting back to me. I was worried in case he was just being nice but a few days later he e-mailed to say that we were on. Better still Sam promised me a two-page spread and asked me to supply him a list of my top five cafes with fifty words on each. We also had a phone interview where I made sure I mentioned my #keepcakeoffserviettes campaign and world record attempt as they both needed some media exposure. He said that they would run the article during the Tour de France as there was obvious synergy.

Still no word from Anglia TV as I felt that I really needed some TV coverage too but I hoped the article in the paper would rekindle their interest.

In the week before my Ironman triathlon event I was meant to be mainly resting (or tapering as we like to call it) but out of the blue Big George contacted me to see if I fancied a ride as he had a surprise. As it was such a beautiful morning I thought I would sneak it in and hope that my Ironman training plan didn't notice. So as not to upset it any further I confirmed that Big George would keep to a leisurely pace, although in his case that isn't normally a problem.

It was also a chance to persuade Big George to be my cycling guest on the trip to find the best café anywhere across Great Britain, literally, so I was on my best behaviour.

An hour or so later Big George turned up ready for the start where he unveiled his surprise. He had only gone and got himself a shiny new bike which he had got for a bargain price off E-bay. This was bad news for me as it meant Big George would be trying to go fast to give his bike a good work out.

He also suggested the Mardlers rest cafe at the Gressenhall museum of Norfolk life as a venue for today as it was very good when he last went.

As predicted Big George set off at a super-fast pace and I was forced to chase after him.

Cycling Guest top cycling tip No. 32. When you get a new bike buy some good quality tyres as the ones that come with it are always cheap and prone to punctures.

Sadly, Big George had not followed Cycling Guest top cycling tip No. 32 and after a few miles we had to stop for him to replace his inner tube. While he fixed it I noted down the puncture on my cycling data spreadsheet which, incidentally, was the 6th cycling guest puncture that year but the first since mid-March. I felt a graph coming on.

After the unplanned stop we set off again with Big George acting like a nine-year-old by putting in lots of fast surges for me to chase down all the way to Gressenhall.

As Big George had recommended the cafe I assumed he knew the way from the museum car park to the café but to my surprise, he told me he couldn't remember as it was over 10 years since he last came. After wandering around for a bit, I was pleased to find the café was still there and thanks to the excellent selection of site maps and signposts we found our way to the entrance.

We went inside and Big George told me he remembered the tiffin being very good but I discovered that sometime in the last 10 years they seemed to have stopped selling it.

You can visit the cafe without having to go into the museum but Big George said the museum was very good. He remembered particularly liking petting the animals in the farm. I felt that it was up to me to break the news to him that the ones he had made friends with on his last visit were now dead.

After a few tears (but no hugging) Big George felt able to set off back to Norwich. This time we had the wind behind so could go extra fast, which seemed to make him forget about his departed farmyard friends and he was soon happy again, enabling me to sign him up for my cross country ride.

Later that week I packed my bike into its box and set off for my Ironman event in Germany.

*****

"How do you know if someone has recently done an Ironman triathlon? You don't have to as they well tell you all about it."

Thanks to all my cake-based training the Ironman Triathlon in Frankfurt went smoothly, apart from the collapsing at the finish and ending up in the medical tent on a drip bit, but that's another story. After a few days' rest I once again felt strong enough to continue my mission.

There would be time for one more ride before my article appeared in the local press. Sam had confirmed the date and that they were busy putting together a map with many of the locations I had been to.

I knew my next post needed to be a good one as anyone attracted to the blog from the article would go to that post first.

For a change and to make sure I maximised interest from all types of cyclists, I decide to introduce some off road into this ride. I had read that you could cycle along the banks of the River Yare all the way from Norwich to Great Yarmouth on the Wherryman's way path. As it had been very dry recently this looked like an excellent opportunity to test it out.

I got up early to put my off-road wheels on to my cyclocross bike and arranged with today's cycling guest, Andrew, for him to bring his mountain bike so that we both had the right kit for the experience.

On leaving Whitlingham we went on a road by the broad and then out through the sewage works before turning off road on to the Wherryman's Way. We soon reached the river where the path was very narrow, muddy and slippery. On one side, there was river and the other a barbed wire fence. This led to that day's cycling guest top cycling tip.

Cycling guest cycling top tip No 34. Before riding along a narrow muddy track with river on one side and barbed wire fence on the other make sure you decide if you would rather get cut or wet as you won't have time to weigh up the choices when you fall off.

Sensibly, Andrew had followed cycling guest cycling top tip no. 34 so when he did fall off his bike he had already chosen the barbed wire fence and therefore only got a cut rather than drowned.

The route next went along a series of nice tracks and we sped along admiring the views, however, as we started to leave civilisation the paths began to get overgrown with stinging nettles and thistles. This may have been ideal country for the likes of Eeyore but I bet he never tried riding his bike though a field this overgrown down in 100-acre woods (or maybe he did and that's why he was always so miserable).

The scratchy paths, plus the very bumpy nature of the rock-hard ground, made going very slow which was not helped when I also got a puncture.

We did get some respite on a nice road section at Surlingham, which gave our wrists and bottoms a chance to recover from the constant vibrations but this flat surface was over far too quickly as we re-joined the river path before enjoying spectacular views of Cantley Sugar beet factory.

Every so often we came across a random river bank gate on the path that seemed to serve no purpose. I was in the lead as we approached the next gate and so stopped to open it. Andrew had not noticed I had come to a halt and with a sudden yelp slammed on his brakes and toppled off the side of the path. Fortunately, he was a bit winded so couldn't immediately get up, giving me enough time to get a photo before checking if he was hurt.

Cycling guest cycling top tip No. 35. To avoid potential injury whilst out on an off-road cycle ride make sure you look where you are going and don't fall off your bike.

Before continuing I held an emergency health and safety executive risk assessment meeting and agreed new random river bank gate health and safety procedures to avoid any further accidents. From now on it would be mandatory to shout 'gate up' when approaching a random river bank gate.

With the new health and safety procedures in place we continued very slowly, but safely, along the path, still being shaken all the way. The path was clearly rarely used as we hardly saw anyone and certainly no wherrymen.

The experience had become quite unpleasant. We therefore decided to cut our losses and turned off the path to head for nearby Loddon.

I had been to Rosy Lee's several times but not for over a year, although it had always been a good stop. As events unfolded over the next 24 hours, ending up here turned out to be a very strange coincidence indeed.

We told the waiter that we would be in the picnic place seating area and gave our order. I went for a hot chocolate and zucchini cake (courgette and lime to you). Andrew went for a pot of tea for one plus carrot cake.

With order placed we were told they would bring it across so we went back outside and wheeled our bikes across the road to the picnic place seating area which was hidden away by the side of Loddon pay and display car park.

Our food and drink was soon delivered to us in a picnic hamper, which I thought was a nice touch. The cake was excellent. In fact, Andrew declared his carrot cake the best he could remember (but he is getting old so that probably only accounts for the last few hours at best).

Fully refreshed we decided to head back home on the roads and stick to tarmac-only trips in future.

*****

I had been told that, subject to there not being any proper news, the article would be published in the EDP today. I nervously thumbed through the pages until I found a double page spread about the cafe cycle Blog.

Not knowing how it would turn out I took a deep breath and I started to read:

He has a passion for two-wheeled adventures and a sweet tooth. He is a man on a mission. Meet East Anglia's Cake Crusader! He runs a popular website reviewing cafes to enjoy while on a bike ride in Norfolk or Suffolk.

A good start although only two sentences in there were already some incorrect facts as I don't have a sweet tooth and it's a blog not a website. However, I shall be pointing out to Barry that the press considers it to be **popular** which is half way to being an internet sensation in anyone's book. I read on:

The former IT manager, who has adopted the guise of the Cake Crusader, began to write down his findings when he decided to branch out from his usual handful of refreshment stops - and soon found an online audience eager for tips.

He started his blog two years ago, and has gone on to review more than 100 cafes, had thousands of people read his reviews and said he was often stopped while out and about by people wanting to talk cycling and cafes.

Strictly speaking I had only been stopped twice but I was very happy with how the article was shaping up as it continued by explaining why I had started the blog, which I knew already, before I hit the jackpot with the closing paragraphs.

He takes his reviews seriously - with a spreadsheet system recording an overall score out of 10, from categories including hot chocolate quality score, guest hot drink score, cake selection and cake quality and atmosphere and ambience score.

As part of his travels he is also completing a survey showing which cafes warm up their cheese scones - as he believes they should be - and which places serve cake on a serviette - which "renders it useless".

Mr Crusader said he was planning a calorie neutral bike ride - to eat slices of cake at 20 cafes cycling eight miles between each one.

This was great as both my cheese scone hot and #keepcakeoffserviettes campaigns now had a media presence but best of all the calorie neutral bike ride was now getting the press coverage it deserved. If you want people to know about a big event, then it doesn't come much bigger than a sentence on page 29 of the local paper.

I thought Sam had done a great job, better than I could have hoped for. The article finished with maps and photos plus mini reviews of my top five cafes. Most importanatly there was the all-important link to the blog.

As soon I was back from the newsagents I checked the count - it had already clocked up 400 visits which set a record for daily visits and it was only breakfast time.

I had previously established the circulation of the EDP is about 50,000 copies a day so worked out that I needed half the readers to visit the blog to reach my target. Despite it being an entertaining and informative article, this was probably a stretch. I would need to cast my media net further and hoped Anglia TV might now get back in touch. To celebrate my breakthrough, I thought a celebratory cafe cycle ride was in order. As yesterday's off-road ride had gone badly wrong I felt it was important to get back to a traditional cafe cycle ride.

Big George was to be the cycling guest but took some persuading as the weather forecast did not look too good for the afternoon. I pointed out that if we set off now we would easily avoid an afternoon soaking, although as it turned out we didn't.

*****

The ride was going well and we had covered about 15 miles. I had made Big George read the article before we set off and had only got it out of my cycling pocket twice more since. I was just putting it away again when I heard my phone ring. It was Mrs Crusader so I thought I better answer. She told me the BBC were trying to get hold of me as they would, subject to there not being any proper news today, like to do a feature on me for tonight's Local news program; Look East.

This was very exciting so I immediately rang the BBC and went straight through to Alex Dunlop, the actual man who does local news reports on the telly. Alex later told me that these days the reporters must find the story, prep the story and edit the story as well as doing the actual reporting to camera bit. I was impressed but then realised it was no different to my blog really. I had to find the café, rate it and take the photos before I got to write the post. The media world is certainly a tough place to inhabit these days.

Alex had seen the article in the EDP and had been working on making it into a news feature whilst he had been trying to get hold of me. I let him know that I was also being chased by Anglia but he scoffed and said the Beeb got a much bigger audience that was sure to help my blog count much more.

He had come up with a plan to film at my current number one rated stop, Earsham Street cafe in Bungay and then go on to his favourite cafe. I explained I was already out on a ride going in the opposite direction but that I was happy to ride over to Bungay to meet him. He was very grateful and, subject to there not being any proper news today, said he would meet me there in a couple of hours' time.

I checked my cycling GPS which said Bungay was about 30 miles away so with a bit of effort I should get there in time. Then I remembered Big George was also with me and he had no idea what was going on. I needed to persuade him to come to but also to go fast. I knew the way to get him to agree was to appeal to his ego as I remembered from his Radio five 'interview' he too was a bit of a media tart. I suggested that his experience from being interviewed on the radio would be invaluable. This seemed to do the trick as Big George had been looking for another opportunity to increase his celebrity status and immediately agreed to the change of plan. I was sure Alex would have enough sense to keep Big George well away from the action and didn't see him as a threat.

We set off again but this time in the opposite direction, on a dash across Norfolk rather impressively arriving at Earsham Street Cafe exactly at the agreed meeting time.

We wheeled our bikes through the cafe to the outdoor seating area where I was proudly directed to my very own reserved table, where Alex joined us to explain the 'storyboard' for the 'shoot' as we like to say in TV.

Through force of habit I had already checked out the cake selection so ordered some vanilla crumble cake and a hot chocolate.

Alex kept insisting on filming our drinks and cake although this didn't seem to affect the taste. Some of the cafe customers asked what was going on. Alex told them he was doing a film about my cycling blog as I was an internet sensation. Yes, he used those actual words. I could have stopped everything there and then because as far as I was concerned my quest was now complete. The BBC had said I was an internet sensation (with less than 30,000 visits at that) and they would know about these things. On reflection, I realised his statement was probably based on the fact the EDP had said it was a popular website and I decided to make sure we avoided the visitor numbers topic.

Using his portable camera Alex continued to film more café action including us going in and out of the cafe with our bikes. With the Earsham Street footage in the can it was off to our next location. Alex said he had arranged for us to go to his favourite cafe which turned out to be Rosy Lees Tearoom. The forecast afternoon rain had now caught up with us as we cycled across to Loddon. There we met up again with Alex who had now been joined by a real cameraman making this into a full-blown film crew. Could it get any more exciting?

We parked our bikes and headed into Rosy Lees where we had some more excellent drinks and cake, which all had to be filmed, before it was time for me to be mic'd up for my in-depth interview on the world of cafe cycle blogging.

The questions were very probing covering all sorts of cake and cycling related issues and I had to be on my toes to make sure I wasn't caught out. I refused to answer any visitor numbers questions, which wasn't too hard as there weren't any. One of the reasons the media were on the lookout for cycling-related stories was because the Tour de France was happening and attracting lots of coverage. I was pleased not to be tripped up on the controversial topic of cake eating on the Tour de France. I am convinced the riders eat cake during the tour and I wasn't afraid to say so on camera.

By the time the interview was over it was pouring with rain but we still needed to film some 'cutaways' of me and Big George cycling with the man off the telly. Alex knew of a good location for this and gave us the directions as he hopped into his car leaving us to get soaked as we followed on our bikes. Halfway there I realised I was still mic'd up and Alex and his cameraman could hear what I was saying. I was worried I could be at the centre of another Gordon Brown style incident. I played back in my mind what I had been talking about in case I had made any inappropriate remarks which would allow Look East to run a very different story; "Bigoted Norfolk cyclist's outrageous cakist views". Much to my relief Big George assured me we had been mainly talking about housework but nice try BBC.

For the 'cutaways' Big George and I had to cycle down to a crossroads where Alex would enter on his bike from stage left. I would then give him a cheery wave and invite him to join us for the ride (I thought my acting was first class). Big George and I then had to cycle behind the camera car and pretend to be chatting about cake and cafes. I clearly acted Big George off the road.

Filming was now complete but I noted the cutaways of us and Alex give the impression he had been out on a long cycle with us. Whereas Big George and I had ridden about 70 miles and got soaking wet, I estimate Alex had done about 70 metres over the course of the day, although that's the magic of TV.

As Alex went off to put his film together we went home to gather our family and friends around the TV to watch the report. I was relieved to see that there had been no proper news that day so the report would get on the show.

We waited patiently and then the presenters introduced the piece. They both had incredulous looks on their faces which had 'was there really no proper news today? Not even a cat stuck up a tree?' written all over them. I can't remember but I don't think they used the words internet sensation but felt it was very much implied. I had contacted Barry to make sure he was watching but he said he would be busy sawing both his legs off so would probably have to miss it.

Alex had put together an excellent item and fortunately most of my interview babble had ended up on the cutting room floor although I noticed the controversial Tour de France cake question had made it in. I thought I had carried the whole thing off rather well but my family and friends seemed to think differently as they rolled around on the floor with mirth. To make matters worse there had been far too much footage of Big George and they hadn't pixilated out his face as I had requested.

My only disappointment was that despite repeatedly bringing up my recent Ironman success throughout the day there was no mention of that or of #keepcakeoffserviettes - but you can't have everything.

The day's publicity jamboree had proved very successful with several thousand additional hits to the blog in one day. This was ten times what I had ever got before and had perhaps put me back on track after all.

Chapter 34
(Visits 39745 only 10255 to go)

The recent media coverage had given me a big boost but the numbers soon dropped off leaving much work still to be done to seal the deal. The next test would be to see how readers of my next post compared to normal. I had also doubled my Facebook numbers and a few more Twitter followers had come on board but would they stick with me?

To find out I went on an emergency short ride to a Norwich café but after posting it attracted no more interest than usual and to add to my woes it looked like August was going to be a bit light on new material with a lack of available cycling guests.

I needed my final two big events to go well if I was to reach my goal. It looked like being a very close-run thing and there were now less than two months to go to judgement day.

World Record attempt planning was also looking a bit chaotic as after my last ride the route had gone to pot and I was back to square one. I had targeted the ride for the start of September giving a few final weeks for the publicity to attract the visitors I needed. Hopefully it would also kickstart the country's ongoing fight against obesity.

There would be time for just one more test ride, and to give a true test I needed to do it at the actual time of the record attempt. It would mean getting up at 5:30am so I set my alarm for an early start.

On my last test ride, with some help from the calorie boffins, I had finally settled on the fact that it takes me approximately five miles to satisfy key rule 6 of calorie neutral bike riding world record rules.

Rule 6. From the time of arriving at the cafe 300 calories must be burnt off before the next cafe can be visited thus making the ride calorie neutral. (300 calories are based on in-depth internet research on average calories of cakes and scones plus average calories of a hot drink (Tea, coffee, hot chocolate).

To accomplish this, I planned a route that wove in and out of Norwich to visit five early-opening cafes before heading out into the country. However, it quickly became apparent that due to city traffic and road furniture I would be well down on my target average speed so would need to go considerably faster than planned once out of Norwich to stick to the timetable.

My opening café was Espresso, in the centre of Norwich. When I arrived, it was only just 7:00am (its official opening time) but it was already up and running. This was a relief so I went inside to satisfy calorie neutral bike riding world record rule 4.

Rule 4 states. *At each cafe, a standard portion of cake or a scone (fruit or cheese) must be consumed. Biscuits, flapjacks, tiffin or anything pre-packaged will not count.*

I now came up against another issue. It being breakfast time there were no cakes or scones (neither fruit nor cheese) available, only Danish pastries, which left me in a quandary. As the self-appointed custodian of the calorie neutral bike ride world record rules, I took the decision to add a subsection to rule 4 which now said that pastries would count as an acceptable cake portion substitute, but only before 9.00am (the end of the official breakfast period) after which they would not be allowed. I thought this was a very fair compromise.

Espresso's hot chocolate and pastry were both excellent and I had no issue in consuming them in under the 12 minutes I had allocated for each cafe visit.

I returned to my bike only to find it had a puncture. I will be on a very tight timescale on the actual day so a puncture would be a serious issue. I changed it as quickly as I could and discovered you burn four calories in the process. This would mean I would have to fix 75 punctures to burn off the necessary calories for the equivalent of a cafe visit, although I didn't have enough spare inner tubes to truly test that theory out.

With puncture fixed the ride round Norwich got a bit chaotic as I nipped in and out of the rush hour traffic. Despite having the route on my bicycling GPS I got lost several times and did not always burn off the requisite 300 calories between stops.

I abandoned the city centre part of the ride as it had been a complete disaster and instead set out to test the new route for the next few cafes on my list. This bit went much better with the next four cafes being visited on schedule.

I had wanted to stop at the final café of the day for a quick refuel but with the skies darkening I decided to head for home before it rained.

I had covered over 60 miles and once again learnt just how difficult it was to plan a calorie neutral bike ride. I had hoped that by now I would have enough information to finalise the route but with no chance of any more practice I cobbled together the best one I could. I had little confidence in my chances of success. Maybe I had bitten off a bit more than I could chew and I didn't just mean the cake.

August had proved to be a frustrating month. Visitor numbers had remained high but I had wanted to make the most of my recent media exposure by doing lots of new rides to follow up on the numerous cafe recommendations I had been receiving. I had been foiled by first the family holiday (where I was only allowed to go on a bike ride twice!), and then a lack of cycling guests. To add to the stress, at the end of the month I was setting off on the start of my 500-mile journey from the Welsh coast to East coast and planning the route and logistics still needed to be completed – which also meant less opportunity for other rides.

Chapter 35
(Visits 43037 only 6967 to go)

The plan was simple, to cycle from St David's in Wales to Lowestoft in England, thus cycling the width of Great Britain, and stopping at cafes along the route to find the best one in order to fulfil the brief.

I had worked out the trip would be about 450 miles and I had allocated five days to cover the distance. Today we would be cycling from the furthest point a bike could reach on the Welsh coast to St Davids which is the most westerly city, a distance of just over 2 miles. But we first had to get to the Welsh coast via 3 trains and a 25-mile ride.

I wanted to do the ride properly which meant adhering to all cafe cycle review rules so I need a cycling guest to help with the reviews and rate the guest hot drink. As it was such a long trip I was pleased that I had persuaded two cycling guests to come along. Not only did it mean that they could help entertain themselves when urgent posting was happening but if I had a guest failure and one couldn't make it all the way then I would have back up. The guests were Big George (who had a proven track record) and Dom who had been to Wales on a lot on family holidays so claimed to be an expert on the region.

Our first challenge was to cycle across London from Liverpool Street Station to catch our next train from Paddington Station. As we were more used to the country lanes of rural Norfolk it turned into a hair-raising team time trial as we were honked at by cars and shouted at by pedestrians but despite a few near misses we just made it to the Newport train on time.

To pass the time, we discussed the training we had each undertaken. I had been able to take Big George on some pre-trip training rides so was confident he would be fine (he wasn't) but it was only now that Dom informed us he had only managed one long ride, of just 70 miles, during which he bonked and had taken several days to recover. After today even our shortest stage would be longer than 70 miles so this didn't bode well.

As we alighted at Newport station everything was still on track. The next leg of the journey was from Newport to Haverford West on a much smaller train. I was concerned about getting the bikes on board as officially the train was only meant to take two and we clearly had three. I became more concerned as our departure platform was strewn with holidaymakers, including another man with a bike. Matters got worse when it was announced that due to a shortage of carriages, our train would only have two carriages instead of the advertised five.

I informed the team of the challenge we were about to face and gave them a train boarding strategy briefing. They were to take no prisoners and everyone was fair game when it came to pushing people out of the way. Dom (old school cyclist) struggled with this concept as he liked to be polite. He was all for waiting for another train or giving up altogether. I had no time for his old-school ways, if we didn't get this train we would not make it to the Welsh coast by nightfall and I was not at home to Mr and Mrs Failure. I told him to man up and get with the programme.

As the train pulled in I skilfully positioned my bike to block the door and then, thanks to some excellent elbow work, I somehow managed to crowbar myself on to the already packed train, leaving hordes of potential passengers on the platform behind. I was relieved to see Big George had piled in right behind me as we wedged the bikes in the gap between the only two carriages.

I looked for Dom but he was nowhere to be seen. Through the window, I could see him helping an old couple and their young grandchildren to board with the bags, buckets and spades they were going to need at the seaside. Amazingly he then manged to pass his bike to us over the heads of the people in the crowded vestibule and squeeze himself on. He looked very smug at having successfully boarded whilst maintaining his Mr Nice credentials.

By the time the guard had spotted us the train was so full that it would have been too difficult to get us and our bikes off again so he just shrugged as he waved his flag and we were off. Every available space on the train was full so it was standing room only for the three-hour journey.

Once we got to Haverford West we were all tired and hungry. Being late afternoon café options were thin on the ground, but after cycling around town for a bit we found Gingers cafe at the Welsh bakery in the centre.

The staff were getting ready to close so the only cake offerings Gingers had left were a custard slice or cream doughnut, neither of which are really cakes. We opted for the cream tea option and I had to award a very low ECS score. Finally, we got on with some actual cycling as we headed out west. The terrain in Wales is not as flat as my cycling guests were used to and despite only travelling 26 miles there were some tired cyclists at the end. With nearly four times further to do tomorrow I realised it could end up being a long day (and it was, much longer than I could have possibly imagined).

We stood and admired the stunning west coast scenery. I also noticed there seemed to be some major building work just offshore but wasn't sure what it was. Luckily, we had our so-called Welsh expert on hand who I could fire my questions at. By using the gift of 'overhearing someone else talking to the lifeboat man', he told us that they were building a new lifeboat station here and the existing one is on the market for half a million Welsh pounds. I was very impressed with his knowledge and looked forward to regular interesting Welsh facts over the next couple of days.

I took a deep breath and looked east thinking about all the adventures the 450 miles between here and seeing the sea again might hold. We sped back along the narrow lane we had just come down but this time we were heading to Lowestoft. It was heads down as we rode for eight minutes and the two miles east to St David's to spend the night. We hadn't exactly broken the back of the ride but at least we were on our way.

As we entered St David's we went past the cathedral which has both a ruined and completed version to cater for all cathedral building tastes (I'm a ruined man). Sadly our so-called Welsh expert couldn't throw much light on how the ruined bit got into that state other then it was probably something to do with dragons, which can be a real problem in Wales.

We located our overnight accommodation and day one was in the bag. With so many potential disasters averted, I felt the search for the best cafe anywhere across Great Britain, literally, was successfully under way and with a bonus cafe review thrown in for good measure. It had also been the riskiest day of the trip as from here it was just a case of cycling the best part of 90 miles for five consecutive days.

Before retiring to bed, I wrote and posted my account of day one as I was desperate for a big blog audience for this trip. While I was distracted my cycling guests snuck off to the pub. I always say what goes on tour stays on the blog so I'm not afraid to report that they drank several pints of local ale and staggered back long after closing time. Not the ideal Preparation for what was to come!

*****

I managed to wake my cycling guests from their deep sleep and waited for them in the breakfast area. I was pleased that they were not too far behind me but breakfast was overly leisurely for my liking. I asked Dom (our so-called Welsh expert) what we could expect of the terrain today. He told us it could be hilly depending on which way we went.

By the time we finally packed up and left we were well behind schedule and soon delayed further when Big George claimed he felt a heavy cold or flu coming on and insisted on finding a chemist.

The first few miles had super views overlooking the sea and we made good progress. To keep us entertained our so call Welsh expert told us several olde Welsh folk tales featuring dragons, lost sweethearts and a mysterious ghostly cyclist who guided lost travellers home wearing only Hi-Viz. Our so-called Welsh expert really seemed to know his stuff.

After about 20 miles it was clear we were going the hilly way as we met many roads with 20% gradient signs. My cycling guests seemed to believe they were now on a hiking rather than biking trip. As I waited for them at the top of the hills they assured me the delays were caused by having to mend punctures. By the end of the day they had apparently had eight between them.

Ten miles further on we arrived at Caffi Beca in Efailven our first official stop on the route. According to our so-called Welsh expert Caffi is Welsh for Café, who'd have thought. There was one table bench outdoors which we decided to use as it was such a nice day.

The staff and customers were all very friendly and seemed worryingly impressed with the fact we were going to Swansea. Comments like, that's hilly, didn't help the already dwindling morale.

The cake selection was disappointing with only Victoria sponge, cupcakes or bara brith (Welsh fruit cake) available. The hot chocolate that Dom and I had wasn't very good but we all had the bara brith which was excellent.

After a few bike adjustments we were off again to Carmarthen hoping there wasn't as much "up" as the locals were predicting (there was). I soon realised that at the bottom of each downhill was a river which was always followed by an uphill. I looked on the map and in the words of UB40 there were many rivers to cross (and apparently 'punctures' to mend) between now and lunch.

We eventually arrived at our planned lunch time stop at nearly 2:30, well behind schedule. Our next cafe to test out was Crumbs cafe in Carmarthen shopping precinct.

It had a continental style outdoor seating area under a big gazebo and inside was a modern looking joint with a satisfying cake selection. They were slightly surprised with my choice of hot chocolate as it was now very hot outside and we all had bright red cheeks but I insisted that it was the right pick for a cyclist. The rest of the team ordered coffee which is also a hot drink but they unfairly avoided any criticism from the staff. To accompany my drink, I had carrot cake but the others just had sandwiches which was an early sign of the mutiny to come.

Once back on the road there was one last long and steep hill, with 'punctures', before the route started to flatten out. There was a worrying development from my cycling guests who started to talk about taking short cuts and changing the route if necessary. I pointed out that, as I had the map and GPS, there was an extremely high probability that we would be going my way.

I had promised one more cafe stop but it wasn't until 5:27pm that I found one which was open. It was called Flanagans coastline cafe in Llanelli. Last orders were at 5:30 so I charged in and ordered before they had a chance to shut.

There was a much better cake selection than at any of the previous venues and the view over the bay was stunning but as they had shut the outside balcony seating area we couldn't take full advantage of it.

Flanagan's coastline café was now top of my table. It may have been the leader in the clubhouse but there were still plenty of other venues out on the course.

We continued along a fantastic flat tarmac off-road path through woods and along the coast until we reached our end point in Swansea.

It had been a very long day and my cycling guests both looked pooped. Big George said he was feeling much worse than this morning and it was definitely flu. He opted for an early night as I updated the blog with today's progress and checked the weather forecast. After the hot and sunny day we had just had, it said tomorrow would be a contrast with heavy rain all day. Big George and Dom started to talk about what we could do if the weather forecast was correct and suggested trains while I pretended not to hear them.

In the morning things were not looking good. I was already in a bad mood as my prediction of how much interest my trip across Great Britain would attract on the blog had proved over optimistic. If only they had Look East in Wales, they would know who I was.

I did have to admit that yesterday Big George had been very poorly. He had decided to see what he felt like after a good night's sleep and then have a fitness test at breakfast before a decision as to if he would take the train for the next section.

While he ate his porridge and made his mind up on his transport choice, I checked the weather which had turned out to be even worse than yesterday's forecast had suggested as it was already raining heavily. This would not only make riding conditions rather tricky but make it harder to persuade my cycling guests to continue the trip on their bikes.

If this wasn't enough then I had an issue with the DI2 wireless gears on my bike. This type of gearing needs a battery to work and I had forgotten to charge it before we left Norwich. It would have been fine if I hadn't decided to leave the charger at home to save weight. There was now a flashing light on the controller insisting that a recharge was required. I didn't know how many more miles the battery had left in it before the gear changer died and I would be stuck in just one cog.

At least Big George's fitness test went well as thanks to drugs and porridge he decided that he was up for the day. Dom (our so-called Welsh expert) and I were both pleased as he had brought the only bicycle pump. I decided not to focus on the rain and hope they didn't notice.

We finally set off with it tipping it down. I kept cheerily suggesting that it was brightening up only to find the rain would then get heavier. My waterproof performed well but I discovered my shoes didn't as I felt my feet sloshing about inside them. A combination of the rain and difficulty in getting through the Swansea and Port Talbot rush hour traffic made progress very slow.

Morale was low as we joined an off-road section at Park Slip nature reserve and after three hours in the wet we were desperate for a break. I asked our so-called Welsh expert where the nearest cafe was and he sarcastically said round the next corner and, to the amazement of all, it was.

It was not the cafe stop I had planned but Park Slip nature reserve coffee shop was a welcome alternative. We parked our bikes and headed straight for the hand driers in the toilet to attempt to dry off and warm up a bit.

Back at the counter we ordered drinks and select cake from the rather small cake selection but they did have a cake of the day, lemon and blueberry, so I chose that.

Although my cycling guests were both very wet and cold, and one was ill, I still insisted they gave their rating input. They reluctantly mumbled some numbers but Park Slip visitor centre cafe didn't surpass the score of our current leader: Flanagans coastline cafe at Llanelli.

Though it was still bucketing down outside we had no choice but to set off again if we were to finish by nightfall so I put my wet coat back on and marched us out to our bikes.

Progress was still painfully slow and I couldn't even raise morale by pointing out the lovely views, probably there but hidden behind the clouds. It was clear that something would have to change if we were going to finish the ride.

It was time for an emergency team meeting under a disused railway bridge. Two options had made it on to the agenda. First was my idea; to speed up and second was the cycling guests' idea; bail out at one of the train stations on the route. By two votes to one the bail out option seemed to be the most popular but I persuaded them to give my speeding up idea a crack if I let them have some lunch.

It seemed a good compromise but it was another hour before we eventually found a cafe in the next big town of Caerphilly.

It was called the Grazing Ground and things got off to a good start when the helpful owners said we could wheel our wet bikes through their cafe into the small outside seating area out back where they would be safe. I suspected most bike thieves wouldn't be out in this weather but we gratefully accepted their offer.

The cake was good and the drinks excellent and the Grazing Ground went straight to the top of the leader board as the current best cafe anywhere across Great Britain, although I think being dry and warm may have helped. With no sign of the rain stopping, Dom and Big George said they felt we had gone far enough by bike today and needed to explore their train option. I didn't want to quit and said that if Big George would lend me his pump I would continue alone.

Just as the whole trip looked like ending in tatters on only the second day, the café cycle gods looked kindly on me. It turned out that there was no 3G phone signal in this part of Wales so train timetables could not be checked. Rather than cycle to the station my cycling guests reluctantly agreed to press on to the next big town before deciding what to do. I did feel a bit guilty as I'm no doctor and Big George looked very drawn and pale. I was sure the last thing he wanted to do was get back on his bike and cycle for another cold and wet 40 miles.

We continued in silence until the outskirts of Newport where we held another team meeting by a roundabout on the ring road. Luckily my cycling guests had pretty much lost the will to live and couldn't face the thought of trying to find the station with all the uncertainty that held. I pointed out that the station nearest to our hotel was 10 miles from it so that option wasn't entirely cycling free either. It was decided that a bailout now sounded like too much hassle and the motion was carried to continue.

This was the turning point as it stopped raining and once round Newport we came across some good flat roads. So, with the use of sports gels, fig rolls and the team time trial skills we had developed in London, we started to race along and make up some of our lost time.

Everything was looking good until we got to the Severn bridge crossing, when the wind picked up and the team faded. By the time we had got across it was rather dark, making the last few miles a real slog to our overnight stop, the Premier Inn just outside Bristol.

I was proud that we had completed the ride as a group, even if we had failed to get three more Welsh cafe reviews done. It also meant I was up well into the night updating the blog with the day's news.

The next day we would start the English leg of the trip but with morale low, limbs stiffening up, general tiredness and bike issues I was far from confident that this trip would get completed. At least the weather forecast looked less watery.

*****

It was to be our 'rest day' as we only had a 'short' 80 miles to do. To help encourage my cycling guests I had promised them some pampering in the Premier Inn spa facilities if we arrived at the hotel on time. My other main mission for the day was to find some charge for my gears as my bike was in increasing danger of becoming a single speed. Yesterday I had refrained from changing gear unless I really had to which had made the ride harder than it need have been (and it had been pretty hard).

Overnight I had attempted to dry my wet things using my bike's secondary function as a clothes-horse but with mixed success, especially in the sock department, as my three available pairs were still all soaking. I climbed back into my wet things before joining the others in the Premier Inn breakfast area.

Over another far too leisurely breakfast cycling guest Dom announced he had a sore knee and said that he had learnt a lot about himself when at his limit on an endurance ride like this. I asked him to list what he had learned: not to cycle too far in one day, not to cycle in the rain and always have a lie in followed by a leisurely breakfast. Most of which seemed unlikely to help us on the rest of the trip.

After missing our 8:00, 8:30 and 9:00 o'clock agreed setting off times we eventually got on the road to Bicester only to discover that the Cotswolds were also full of hills, not as steep as Wales but they went on for longer. This made for another tough morning of cycling.

As we passed through Nailsworth Dom spotted Cafe 28. This was too good an opportunity to miss as not only was it a chance to review the first English cafe but it would also count towards one of my other projects: of visiting all cafes named 1 to 100 and I hadn't got a 28. I later discovered there was also a Café 28 in Norfolk, which I have since visited. I now have a swap which I am happy to exchange with any other collectors of cafes named 1-100.

No. 28 was a small cafe over two floors with the addition of a couple of outside pavement tables where we chose to sit so we could keep an eye on the bikes.

For the second day running I had lemon and blueberry cake while Dom again had some peanut slice (an expensive Snickers bar). Big George was still not feeling 100% so wanted something savoury before choosing a croissant.

A small boy with his grandfather started to admire our bikes. He was getting very excited with one particular feature. It was not my state of the art albeit uncharged electronic gears, nor Dom's lovely carbon frame but the fact Big George's bike had two water bottle holders rather than one. He clearly has much to learn.

I felt my hot chocolate was a bit too Cadbury's but still nice, Dom enjoyed his coffee and Big George his cup of tea. Our cakes were also good if not exceptional so Cafe 28 scored well and moved into second place in my search. It had set a good standard for the English cafes to beat.

After another couple of hours we got to the next stop. Here we discovered that Cirencester was the world capital of cafes and tea shops, having one every few yards. If you were the sort of sad person who has nothing better to do with their time than write a café blog then Cirencester would keep you busy for many years.

We choose Jacks cafe for our lunch break. It was packed so we had to start off in the drizzle on an outside table until an inside one became free.

There was a very good cake selection but once again Big George passed on any while I had a huge slice of coffee and walnut and Dom a brownie. Drinks and cakes were good so with high scores all round Jacks went into the lead as the best café.

Before we left Cirencester we found a bike shop where I persuaded a bemused owner to charge my gears for 30 mins to give them the boost required to get me home. Meanwhile Dom took the opportunity to buy and fit replacement brake blocks as his had worn thin during all our many descents. Big George was furious about how long we were spending at the bike shop as it was eating into his potential spa pamper time.

Once the Cotswolds were behind us the terrain got much flatter and we could pick up the pace and even practice our team time trial skills again. It was only now we noticed we had forgotten to refill water bottles at lunch so needed a shop, but it became apparent that all Oxfordshire villages only contain posh stone houses and no shops. It was quite different in Wales where there was a post office and shop on every street corner.

With parched throats we entered the small town of Wittney and looked for a cafe but here the town seemed to contain only pubs. I could tell Big George and Dom would have much preferred to go in one of them but I couldn't let that happen, as it would not be fulfilling the cafe brief. So I cycled round Wittney town centre until I eventually found an actual coffee shop and demanded that they join me.

It was now 4:45pm and the Coffee Shop shut at 5:00pm. I asked the lady if they were still open. She couldn't have been more disappointed to see a customer at this time of day if you had paid her. She clearly wanted to say no but it was marginally too early so she reluctantly got me a hot chocolate and some tiffin while Dom had tea and flapjack. Big George wanted a sandwich but the lady said they stopped making them at 4:30pm so he went to the Co-op instead.

Neither of our drinks or cakes was very good and you could feel the chill from the lady as she waited to lock up. This was certainly not the best cafe anywhere across Great Britain or probably even in Wittney.

We left for a final 20-mile push but despite good progress we got to the hotel well into the evening and much too late for my cycling guests to be pampered in the Premier Inn spa, even if they had had one.

Today's ride may have taken a lot longer than planned but there had been little rain plus we had also managed to get our bikes back into good working order. I believed that my tough cycling love had started to pay off, as had our new-found team time trial skills. Big George had even put in some excellent surges, which blew the peloton apart, and Dom also went for an outrageous break away (while me and Big George had been distracted taking off waterproofs). Once caught, he claimed he had turned himself inside out and gone to some very dark places. This is the type of cycling chat I wanted to hear and a much-improved turnaround from earlier in the week.

There was no more talk of bail out options and there were even suggestions that we set off early and forgo the very leisurely breakfast to put some miles under our belts first thing tomorrow. We could still complete this mission yet.

Chapter 36
(Visits 43452 only 6548 to go)

There were just two days to go to complete the search for the best café across Great Britain but disappointingly there was still a lack of interest on the blog. Numbers were up on previous long adventures but not at the breakthrough levels I needed to become an internet sensation. Today we would be re-entering the Look East TV region so hopefully things might pick up again.

After yesterday's "easy day" I had planned over 100 miles for us today. To get to the hotel before nightfall an early start would be required. It had been my turn for the single room so I had little confidence of this happening. When I wheeled my bike out of the lift for our 7.00 am meet up, I was both pleased and surprised to find that my two cycling guests had got there before me. Last night I had given each team member two bananas and some instant porridge to provide our early morning fuel. They claimed to have dutifully eaten it so without further ado we were ready for the off.

Out on the road it took a while for our legs to wake up but once in our stride we were bombing along to the first planned stop at Bletchley. As we had missed our normal overly leisurely Premier Inn all you can eat breakfast I had promised my cycling guests we would stop at a cafe that does a good fried breakfast instead. Although I'm not a big fan of a full English I had done some internet research and Mister Tea's seemed to fit the bill.

We arrived just before 9:00am and headed inside. To my horror there were numerous different fry up options but no cakes. I had feared that this might be the case but went along with it for the good of team morale. However, if I was going to give it a cafe cycle review then the only option for me was some slightly stale chocolate chip shortbread, which isn't even really cake. I have had problems before getting cake at cafes early in the morning but with my recently introduced pre-breakfast cake flexibility rule I would be all right.

To show willing I also ordered a medium fried breakfast to go with my hot chocolate and slightly stale chocolate chip shortbread. Big George was next to order and put me to shame by putting in a poached egg on toast foundation (totally off menu) around which he then skilfully constructed a fry up masterpiece. I clearly have much to learn on the fried breakfast front so I will continue to focus on cake.

There was a huge difference of opinion between me and my cycling guests over the rating of this cafe. For me Mister Tea's rated poorly on my hot chocolate and cake based system but Big George and Dom felt the whole experience was fantastic. I reminded them that it's my blog and scoring system so I'm afraid Mister Tea's found itself in last place.

With a very happy set of domestiques, we quickly covered the next 20-mile part of the day's stage into Bedford where I took them to Frescos, a cafe much more to my taste.

Frescoes has a big copy of a Michelangelo fresco above the door although no explanation as to why. It was a nice feature to study while sitting in the pleasant outdoor seating area just off Bedford High Street.

Inside there was a good cake selection to choose from but despite this Big George ordered a Danish pastry when he knew it had gone 9:00am and that my pre-breakfast cake flexibility rule no longer applied. He also ordered a smoothie, which does not qualify as a guest hot drink what with it not being hot. It was almost as if he was deliberately ordering things so he did not have to take part in any cycle cafe rating.

Fortunately, Dom, my back up cycling guest, was still prepared to play along (at least for now) and had a latte and chocolate fudge cake. I had the house speciality of black forest gateaux.

Despite the cake portion being rather on the small side the cakes were excellent and our drinks the best all week, so far. Thus, Frescos leapt to the top of the best cafe across Great Britain leader board.

The next part of the ride was 35 miles across the flatlands of Cambridgeshire. Apparently, Cambridgeshire has the lowest highest point of any county in Great Britain so I was confident that we wouldn't be having any more tough climbs for quite a while. This was good as I had discovered the team were now very good at cycling as long as it was flat or downhill making this terrain much more to their liking. We sped along in our now highly-drilled formation.

As I knew there was little civilisation on this part of the route I suggested we had an unscheduled stop at Waresley Park garden centre cafe. Despite this being another potential cycle cafe review stop even I couldn't face a third hot chocolate so soon after the last one and had a cup of tea instead. I also fuelled up on a cheese scone and fruit cake, while Dom and Big George had sausage rolls and water. Although the refreshments were rather good we didn't cover enough of my café cycle reviewing categories to rate the place so it will go down in cafe cycle history as the stop that never was.

Refuelled we flew along the cycle friendly flat roads to the university town of Cambridge. After all the problems in the first few days we were a cycle team at last, or so I thought.

Because of my TV appearance I was getting more recommendations of cafes and tea shops to try and one such suggestion was Michaels House in Cambridge, situated in an old chapel- like building with tables also available outside.

Once seated it became clear that my cycling guests had lost all interest in cakes and ordered pizza and salad with a cup of tea. They seemed to have forgotten what this trip was all about.

I did at least get them to help rate the atmosphere and ambiance score, which was high due to the seating options, setting and very pleasant staff. My hot chocolate was by far the best of the week and the scone and brownie I went for were excellent too. It was just a shame that my guests only went for a cup of tea because, as you may recall, the most a cup of tea can score is 7.

Despite this Michaels House jumped straight to the number one spot in my cafe search. I eagerly reported the news on Twitter. Dom suggested that people would be upset or call foul if after going all the way to Wales the winning café was one within my normal catchment area. I was pleased to see I had finally sucked him into my world. If only I had brought Barry on the trip.

When I eventually managed to persuade my cycling guests back on to the bikes things took a downturn. As tiredness set in, we crossed the border to the hillier Suffolk countryside where the team once again fell apart. Big gaps started to appear between the riders, our average speed dropped and the happy banter turned to silence, as the last few miles became a real slog.

When we finally made it to our destination, a hotel by a roundabout just outside Bury St Edmunds, I was very surprised to find that our longest ride had turned into our earliest finish. Although my team were slumped half asleep in the bar I was now confident of completing the last 58 miles tomorrow.

To celebrate we enjoyed a drink. I felt this was the right moment to introduce one final twist. I told the team that I had to finish the ride by 1pm tomorrow to get to an urgent appointment. I was surprised how well the news went down although I suspected that they were just desperate to get home and not have to eat any more cake. This would once again mean a 7am start and no breakfast. At best, we would only have time for one more cafe stop. Big George immediately voted for this to be at Morrisons, as they did a good fried breakfast. I agreed that was a possible option (but it was never really going to happen).

*****

After five hard days in the saddle we set off for the procession into Lowestoft. I did warn them that if we started to slip behind schedule we would need to put the hammer down (cycle speak for go faster) which they appeared to understand.

I took the lead and kept up a decent pace as we raced through the deserted roads of Suffolk and Norfolk. At 7.00am on a Saturday morning there was not much traffic about so despite riding into the wind I felt progress was acceptable to meet my deadline. After about 20 miles I was surprised when cycling guest Dom wanted to confirm that I had put the hammer down early as he was starting to feel the pace. I explained that the size of hammer used so far was like the tiny one used by the shoemaking elves and if we were to put the hammer down properly it would be more like the one belonging to mighty Thor and he would know all about it. Once again, my morale boosting skills seemed to do the trick and we arrived at the scheduled cafe, the Angel just outside Diss, right on time.

Despite it still being early it was important to have cake to give the Angel a crack at the best cafe across Great Britain title. I was impressed at what was available at this time in the day so awarded a good ECS rating. I went for fridge cake.

My cycling guests were now refusing to eat any more cake whereas this was my 13th piece of the week. They insisted on fried breakfast and a pot of tea making their input virtually useless.

My hot chocolate was nice and my fridge cake was excellent so good scores all round but not enough for the Angel Cafe to take the title. The only downside was this was the first cafe this week that had served my cake on the serviette. Particularly disappointing seeing as I was now back on home turf where my #keepcakeoffserviettes had been most visible. Maybe it's just an East Anglian thing.

Coincidently, the previous week I had a comment on my blog from someone who had been unimpressed with one of my top ten cafe recommendations, as they had had to wait 20 mins for their coffee and scone to arrive. Their comment had gone on to recommend that I try the Angel at Diss, (where we were). It was therefore somewhat ironic that we were on the wrong end of some big breakfast orders and had a longer wait than my correspondent had had for his coffee and scone. Not normally a problem on such a nice day but on this day, it was starting to threaten my deadline. The friendly owner was very apologetic and gave us a complimentary pot of tea to make up for our wait, which only delayed us further.

After finishing the free tea we were off again knowing that we couldn't drop the pace even though the wind had picked up. Everyone dug deep and when I once again applied the shoemaking elves tiny hammer. They responded well and we made it to our point furthest east, in Lowestoft, right on schedule.

I checked the cycling stats to find we had covered 470 miles and visited 13 establishments in my search to find the best cafe anywhere across Great Britain, literally. I was impressed with the way my cycling guests had kept going to the end. I was less impressed with their cafe rating performance, which had been extremely disappointing, especially in their cake eating and guest hot drink rating role.

As well as finding the best café anywhere across Great Britain, literally (won by Michaels House cafe in Cambridge) the trip was excellent training for my calorie neutral cycle ride world record attempt, which was now less than three weeks away. Although my visitor rate had remained higher since being on TV I would still need a final spike to hit the required total. Everything would now depend on getting the extra publicity I needed.

*****

I contacted the local paper again and much to my surprise they were more than happy to run a piece on the calorie neutral cycle ride world record attempt. I was even more surprised that they were going to send a photographer along as well to make it into a proper news story. But would this be enough?

I suspected not, so on world record eve I decided to write to the Ken Bruce show on BBC radio 2 with the following.

"Hi Ken,

I see today the new Guinness book of so-called world records is out. Well tomorrow I'm planning to set the world record for a calorie neutral cake and bike ride. Basically, I need to go to as many cafes as possible on my bike and have a cake and hot drink at each. The only rule is you must burn off the calories from the last visit before you can go to the next. I plan to do 20. This will help prove to my disbelieving friends that cake and exercise are perfect bedfellows.

Well I wrote to the Guinness book of so called world records about my forthcoming attempt and they washed their hands of me, as they don't do gluttony records, which this clearly isn't. Who needs them anyway, as I'm quite capable of making my own world record certificate using my colouring set.

I have trained hard on the bicycling bit but really need an expert on eating to advise on the cake eating part, are you free to advise?
Thanks
The Cake Crusader"

After sending it in I set off to drive up to Andrew's house for one last ride before the big day. I put the car radio on and waited for

Ken to read out my e-mail as it was clearly the best he would be getting today. Then, much to your surprise, after two records he announced that he had been contacted by the Cake Crusader and read the whole thing out.

Straight away my phone was red hot and by the time I arrived at Andrew's I found myself at the centre of a media storm having received both an e-mail and a tweet from people who had heard Ken's show. I had to delay the start of our ride (by almost a minute) as I dealt with all the necessary social networking before we could set off.

I returned home to rest up before the big day. Normally before an endurance event you would have a big pasta tea but as I needed to fit in twenty slices of cake I just had cabbage soup.

Chapter 37
(Visits 45048 only 4952 to go)

After a sleepless night, the alarm had gone off very early so I crawled out of bed and prepared for the big day.

First, I reread what I thought would be the final set of calorie neutral bike ride record attempt rules (they weren't) as they had changed several times and I didn't want to fall foul of any of them and get disqualified.

1. The holder of the record will have visited the highest number of different cafes during a single day.
2. All cafes must be independent and not part of national chains
3. All cafes must be visited within their normal opening hours and not open early or kept opened late for a record attempt
4. At each cafe a standard portion of cake or a scone (fruit or cheese) must be consumed. Biscuits, flapjacks, tiffin or anything pre-packaged will not count.
   4.1 Danish style pastries are acceptable but only during the breakfast part of the day, before 9.00am, as cakes are not always available
5. At each cafe a standard hot drink must be consumed. (Tea, coffee or hot chocolate). If served in a pot or jug than one cup's worth must be drunk.
6. From the time of arriving at the cafe 300 calories must be burnt off before the next cafe can be visited thus making the ride calorie neutral. (300 calories are based on in-depth internet research on average calories of cakes and scones plus average calories of a hot drink (Tea, coffee, hot chocolate).
7. If extra calories have been used up between cafes then that is tough, as they cannot be credited against other legs of the ride.
8. Calories burnt to be counted on a generic calorie counting device using only cycle speed, rider weight and age to

calculate calorie usage. No heart rate or power consideration is required.

With the rules burnt into my brain I reminded myself of the work undertaken to generate maximum coverage as I really needed lots of visits off the back of this one. My publicity department had done a fine job publicising the event with the mention on the Ken Bruce show plus a one-page article in the local paper (the next day). I also aimed to update my followers with tweets during the day. But with all this local and national coverage the pressure was now on.

I got my bike out of the garage, hopped on it and with a deep breath started my timer and calorie counter. I had my triathlon Garmin 910XT watch (yes, the same one I used in the Ironman triathlon I did recently in case I hadn't mentioned it) to measure calorie consumption and my Garmin Edge 810 to show me the route whilst recording time and mileage.

The first part of the ride was a now well-rehearsed circuit of five cafes in and around Norwich which all opened nice and early, starting with Expresso in the centre of town.

When I arrived, I checked my calories only to find my Garmin said I had only burnt 270 calories getting there. This meant that I had to do a quick extra loop up and down the road before dashing in to have a hot chocolate and Danish pastry (see rule 4.1). I hoped I hadn't got the calorie count wrong for every bit of the route or my timings would be completely off. I was already starting to feel the pressure. I had little contingency built in but if I started to slip too much from the schedule the later cafes would be shut before I got there.

At each café I was allowed 12 minutes to order, consume cake and drink the drink and I completed the first one in under 10 minutes. It was nice to have had a pleasant if not leisurely breakfast and to have some food inside me. I set off again now feeling good, two minutes ahead of plan and only 19 more cakes to eat. How hard could this be?

It was a lovely sunny morning and the ride continued smoothly as I now seemed to have my calorie count and route distances back in sync as I did a five-mile loop to Warings café before cycling up to the Britannia cafe overlooking Norwich.

My next stop was Pandora's Kitchen where I was due to meet the press photographer. He would be taking the photo, which would appear on the coveted page 36 slot of the EDP next day. Pandora's Kitchen is always a high quality and very friendly stop and the team there were pleased to see I had made it on time. I ordered a salted caramel brownie and pot of tea. (I had previously worked out it was always best to have a pot and not a mug at each stop as per rule 5 you only need to drink one cup and tea cups are much smaller).

The salted caramel brownie was my favourite cake of the day, not only delicious but early enough on the route that I was still enjoying cake.

While eating and drinking was happening the press photographer was trying to do his photo shoot. We tried several poses of different cake and bicycle combinations until he was happy. My only concern was to make sure that in any photo my Ironman race number sticker would be clearly visible on my helmet.

The extra time needed to pose for photographs meant I blew my 12-minute slot and was now running late so needed to pedal extra hard to my next stop which was Stephanie's just a few minutes from Crusader Towers. Here I was met by Mrs Crusader, who had wheeled me down a different bike, so I could swap from my more manoeuvrable city bike to my time-trial bike for the rest of the route (I've seen this done on the Tour de France, but without the tea and cake).

With the aid of my faster steed I could make up some time as I arrived at Acorn tearooms in Poringland for another pleasant and successful stop.

Then it was on to the Cafe in Brooke where I was joined by my support team, Mrs Crusader and Peter (student son), who had come along on the promise of free food. They would drive to each cafe to meet me with my spare bike and offer words of encouragement like, don't you feel sick yet?

Knowing that I would be tweeting progress all morning I was worried that I could have gone viral by now. This could mean that large crowds might start to gather and potentially slow my progress. Thanks to my meticulous preparation I had a plan for this possibility and had asked my friend John to join us as he owns a motorcycle. He had agreed to provide an escort through the potential crowds.

John turned up on time so as we left the Café at Brooke he took the lead with me following behind, far enough back to avoid any calorie sucking slipstreaming. He led me through the imaginary crowds all the way over to Rosy Lees tea room in Loddon for another quick tea and cake stop.

It appeared that I hadn't gone viral after all as the roads were free of cheering crowds so John decided his services probably weren't needed after all and went home again as he said he had better things to do with his time. I, on the other hand, didn't, so I set off to the next stop was Every day's a picnic (EDAP) cafe at Hedenham, where I would normally have the award-winning chocolate and Guinness cake, but today the smaller banana cake looked more appropriate so I stuck with that along with a single cup of tea from a generous pot.

It was now down to Bungay and the number one rated Earsham street cafe. I surprisingly arrived bang on scheduled time at 12:53pm. I thought this was rather impressive especially as I was now half way, but it was the last time I kept to my schedule for the rest of the attempt.

My support team had already got there and were tucking into bacon sandwiches and sausage rolls, both of which looked very nice and a rather more enjoyable lunch than the cake and hot chocolate I had planned.

I was feeling fine from a cycling viewpoint but had to confess that I was now struggling on the cake eating front and I no longer felt I could just stuff the cake down within the twelve-minute window. I would need to take more time at the cafes, which would eat into my timetable.

I set off late towards Harleston where I was not aware of the drama that was about to unfold and potentially derail the whole event.

No.5 at Harleston had no social media presence and so I had been unable to inform them of my mission. The lack of on-line information was explained when, on arrival, I discovered the cafe had shut down.

Luckily, there are lots of other cafes in Harleston and so, despite having never been there before, I headed to the nearest one. For reasons that will become apparent, I will not be naming the cafe or ever planning to return, as it was the worst cup of tea I can remember and the cheese scone was almost inedible.

I tried my best to force it down but the unpleasant taste and dryness made it very difficult especially considering how much cake I had already eaten. I ate as much as I could before I hid the last few small pieces under the butter wrapper.

Now feeling rather ill it was off to the Pennoyer centre at Pulham St Mary where I knew I would be getting excellent cake baked by one of the ladies from the village. On arrival, my support team were already soaking up the afternoon sun as I went inside to order a cup of tea and request the smallest slice possible of the apple and raisin cake.

The cake was excellent and restored my confidence in being able to complete the eating part of the task although looking at my watch I was now running over 20 minutes late. If I continued to leak time at this rate, then the later cafes on the list would definitely be closed before I got to them. I hatched a plan with my support team to speed things up at the next stop and hit the road again to ride up to Goodies cafe at Pulham Market.

When I got there Mrs Crusader had already pre-ordered my tea and cake, which I could scoff straight away in less than five minutes, I checked the rules and they said nothing about who could order the cake. Despite the few minutes I made up here I lost further time at the visits to the Tudor Bakehouse in Long Stratton and the Garden Tearoom in Wymondham getting there with only minutes to spare before they closed.

I still had five cafes to go but was feeling rather queasy, unfortunate when you need to pick up the pace to set the calorie neutral café cycle ride world record. I got back on the bike and attempted to put the hammer down (of the Thor variety) on the ride over to Hingham. Not only did I fail to claw back anytime but I was greeted with my next potentially terminal challenge.

My target cafe was Lincoln's by the village green but on arrival my support team informed me it was closed. I knew that on a Friday and Saturday evening Lincoln's reopens again as a Bistro. As today was a Friday and almost 5 o'clock I guessed it would reopen soon.

My plan to keep things on track was to swap the cafe with my other Hingham venue of Chalfonts, which I had planned to visit in two cafes time. I was sure that on my return to Hingham, at approx. 6:30pm, I would be able to go to the now open Lincoln's Bistro where I assumed they would still give me a cup of tea and some cake even in Bistro mode. I was very pleased that potential disaster had been averted, or so I thought. I waved off my support team as Peter (student son) had had enough free food and had had a better offer of how to spend his Friday evening.

The closed cafe incident had delayed me further and in all the excitement I asked for a cup of tea instead of a pot. It was a simple mistake to make but resulted in a huge mug of brew. I had had so much tea already today that drinking it took me a lot longer than my allotted twelve minutes.

With the world record starting to slip away I slumped down in my chair and started to think about giving up. I would need to cycle much faster and then get the cake and drink down quicker than the lack lustre performance I was currently putting in. The thought of a gloating Barry or Duncan telling me it was time I found something better to do with my time made me determined. I knew that if I fell any further behind then I would have to call the attempt off and admit defeat. So, despite having already cycled over 100 miles, I somehow managed the strength to ride to Yaxham Waters cafe doing it 15 minutes quicker than planned.

I was very impressed with myself but on closer examination of the timetable I realised I had miscalculated and allowed a ridiculously long time for this leg of the ride by mistake. For once an error had fallen in my favour and meant that it might just be possible to get around the remaining cafes before the last one shut. It would still take some extra fast cycling, eating and drinking but it was worth continuing. Most importantly I would need Lady Luck to stay on my side.

Unfortunately, she appeared to have popped down the shops, as luck was nowhere to be seen when I ordered my next round of tea and cake. As it was late in the day Yaxham Waters only had one cake left, a giant Victoria sponge which took a lot of effort to work through being my 17th, and possibly largest, piece of cake that day.

As the last few cafes would be the hardest I would be joined by Jim (ex-work colleague) to help keep up morale. Jim still worked in big business and often got sent on team building type courses meaning he could encourage me with the motivational sayings he had been taught. As I struggled with the Victoria sponge he helpfully pointed out that even the longest journey starts with a single piece of cake.

Once I had finally finished the cake it was back to our bikes as we returned to Higham. As my legs started to turn to jelly Jim kept me going: "when in doubt, pedal it out" and "pain is temporary but quitting lasts forever". I quickly learnt that if I showed any weakness then Jim would instantly hit me with another inspirational statement, which were making me feel sicker than the cake sloshing around in my stomach. It was less painful to get my head down and cycle as fast as I could back down the road.

Once back in Hingham I was pleased to see I had completed that section in the time allowed. I was less pleased to discover that Lincolns was still shut despite it being thirty minutes after the advertised Bistro opening times. I had to think fast to keep the record going. I checked the calorie neutral bike ride world record official rules and decided there may be some ambiguity I could exploit. It wasn't clear if a cafe could be visited twice during a record attempt. To clarify this I decided to insert rule 1 subsection 1 which now stated:

"If on arrival at a planned cafe stop the cafe is closed, despite it being at time contained within the 'café's clearly advertised opening times, then a previously visited cafe may be revisited as long as it is within 1 mile's radius of the closed cafe. In no other circumstances, can a cafe be visited more than once during a world record attempt"

As luck would have it my situation exactly matched the circumstances described in rule 1.1 and as Chalfonts was within the 1-mile radius laid out in the ruling I was able to return there with the record attempt still intact. Lady Luck was clearly back home.

By now Mrs Crusader had returned in the support car, so to celebrate my good fortune I bought Jim a cup of tea and her a bag of BBQ hula hoops.

With time still pressing I thanked Jim for his support but decided he had inspired me enough for one day so left him and my support team discussing if Monster Munch or Hula Hoops are the potato based snack of choice as I charged back towards my penultimate stop with the clock ticking away far too quickly.

I arrived at Janey's Village cafe to be met by Dom who had come to join me for the final leg. However, before we could tackle that there was the small matter of more tea to be drunk and cakes to be eaten here.

I thought a fruit scone would be easier to eat at this point but this proved another cake selection error as the world's biggest fruit scone turned up. It took some time to finish as it piled itself up on top of the previous 18 cakes already consumed.

By the time I was ready to set off again it was dark. There were just five miles to go before the final stop at the Station Bistro Wymondham so with no lights on my bike I was glad of the help from Dom's bike lights to help guide us there safely.

It had been a struggle but I was mighty relieved to climb off the bike with the cycling part of the record completed. I just needed to have one more piece of cake and the record was mine. As we went inside I had my final piece of good fortune as the waitress said they had been going to close early, having run out of customers, when someone turned up meaning they had stayed open a bit longer. It was clear that to break a world record luck has to be part of your team.

On the counter was a rather fine-looking fruit cake which (incredibly) I really fancied. I bought myself and Dom a cup of tea and I had the fruit cake. Dom declined any cake saying he had had some at Janey's village cafe and was now full. I decided that Dom probably won't be a threat to my world record in the future.

With the final cup of tea drunk and cake eaten my work for the day was done. The support team drove us back to race HQ where I decided to put celebrations on hold while I slumped in front of the telly feeling just a little sick before going for a lie down.

For calorie neutral bike ride world record attempt fans here are the ride stats. I cycled 126 miles, spent 9 hrs 38 mins on the bike and 4 hrs 24 mins in cafes burning 8267 calories while consuming about 6000.

After the ride, I immediately decided to never try and repeat the feat again so if anyone ever wants to break the record then fill your boots and I will make and send you a homemade world record certificate if you are successful.

There was just one month to go until Barry's deadline. Could I extract enough interest to get the required number of people to make me into an internet sensation?

Chapter 38

It had now been exactly two years since I had posted about my first café cycle so by the terms of Barry's bet time was up. I had agreed to meet up with him and present the final figures. I hadn't looked at the blog for the last week so neither of us knew if I was an Internet sensation or not. The last count I had was still several hundred short. We agreed to meet at the corner house café in Mundesley, which had been the subject of my very first post, and check the count on my phone.

Duncan had already had to admit defeat as to whether my blog is an aid to cutting the obesity epidemic in this country so I was hoping for a second win here.

Visitor numbers had certainly increased markedly mainly thanks to my piece on the BBC local news (both evening and night time slots) plus the interest generated from my success at becoming the world record holder for most cafes visited on a calorie neutral bike ride. Since then my last few posts had done particularly well, but would it be enough?

I thought again about everything I had done on my quest

I had written 204 posts
Organised 16 group rides
Visited over 200 cafes
Been on 4 rides recommended by cycling celebrities
Had coverage in the local paper, on local TV and national radio
Cycled to Paris
Spread the word of café and cake to Europe
Cycled across Great Britain (literally)
And became a cycling and cake eating world record holder

We arrived at the corner house café and parked our bikes. I ordered a medium hot chocolate, as they still hadn't got any large cups, but as usual Barry stayed clear of any potential recognition of café cycle reviewing by having a coke and a sausage sandwich. Then we were ready.

I nervously got my phone out and loaded the blog before scrolling down to the count and there it was 50,017. I had not only become an internet sensation but by more than 17 views, what a result.

Barry was shocked and demanded a recount (which also came to 50,017) before reluctantly having to admit he had lost. I made him agree that he was wrong to have ever questioned the idea that people would not be interested in a cycling and cake fusion blog. He did say he felt vindicated as most internet sensations do it by posting an amusing clip of their pet on a skateboard whereas I had dug a lot deeper to reach my goal. He suggested that it is more of an overnight thing rather than a two-year campaign so he decided he had been far too generous with the terms of our bet.

But there was no getting away from it: he had lost and I was now officially an internet sensation (I felt a homemade certificate coming on). The only disappointment was the lack of humble pie on the menu for him to enjoy. "I assume you are going to stop this nonsense and find something better to do with your time?" he grumpily said as he tucked into his sausage sandwich.

"I've still only scratched the surface" I said. "My work will not be done until all local cafes are reviewed, cheese scones are always warmed and cake is never served on its serviette again".

"Oh". He said, "I was rather hoping we could go back to cycling to the pub" (but we haven't).

Acknowledgements

Thanks to the many cycling guests who accompanied me on all the rides I undertook by humouring me as I insisted on photographing and scoring every cake and drink they had.

I'm especially grateful to Andrew (who remains notoriously hard to please), Big George, Dom and Barry and Helen and their Tandem as my chief cycling companions who have taken the brunt of most of my 'observations'.

Also thanks to all the cafes that I have visited without which there would have been no book and who always seem to take my light-hearted comments in the way I intended. If I mentioned you by name in the book then you are one of my favourites.

A huge thanks to Annie for volunteering to edit the book. She did a fantastic job of turning my ramblings into something coherent. Without her help I don't think I would have got it into a state I would have ever been happy with.

My biggest thanks goes to my wife Chris for her continued patience as I set off on yet another ride, ongoing support by always reading my posts and encouragement by reading the drafts and giving me the feedback I needed. I couldn't have done it without you.